D0595315

SPIRITUALITY
and Recovery

Also by Leo Booth

The Wisdom of Letting Go

Say Yes to Your Life

Say Yes to Your Sexual Healing

Say Yes to Your Spirit

The Angel and the Frog

The Happy Heretic

SPIRITUALITY and Recovery

A Classic Introduction to the Difference
Between Spirituality and Religion
in the Process of Healing

A Guide to Positive Living
Fourth Edition

LEO BOOTH

Health Communications, Inc.
Deerfield Beach, Florida

www.hcibooks.com

Unless otherwise noted, all Scripture quotations are taken from the Good News Translation in Today's English Version—Second Edition. Copyright © 1992 by American Bible Society. Used by permission. Scripture quotations marked KJV are taken from the King James Version of the Bible. (Public Domain.) The author has added italics to Scripture quotations for emphasis.

Library of Congress Cataloging-in-Publication Data

Booth, Leo, 1946–
Spirituality and recovery : a classic introduction to the difference between
    spirituality and religion in the process of healing : a guide to positive
    living / Leo Booth.—4th ed.
        p. cm.
    Includes bibliographical references.
    ISBN 978-0-7573-1702-6 (pbk.)
    ISBN 0-7573-1702-2 (pbk.)
    ISBN 978-0-7573-1703-3 (ebook)
    ISBN 0-7573-1703-0 (ebook)
    1. Recovering addicts—Religious life.   2. Recovering alcoholics—
Religious life.   3. Spirituality.   4. Religion.   5. Healing—Religious
aspects.   I. Title.
    BL625.9.R43B66 2012   204.42   12/12
    204'.42—dc23   B   SEBCO
                                            1295

                                                                        2012016885

Publisher: Health Communications, Inc.
          3201 SW 15th Street
          Deerfield Beach, FL 33442-8190

Cover design by Dane Wesolko
Inside book design and formatting by Dawn Von Strolley Grove

Maud and Len Booth,

Loving and supportive parents.

Contents

Acknowledgments

TO DEVELOP A POSITIVE lifestyle, it is helpful to be surrounded by special people who, by their love, support, and practical criticisms, enable the journey of life to be made. In the writing of this book, I have specifically appreciated Gloria Coker, who, with few guidelines from the author, created such wonderful sketches. And numerous colleagues and friends who, in the dropping of a word, created a story line.

I'm grateful.

Introduction

THIS REVISED EDITION OF *Spirituality and Recovery* attempts to explain the important distinction between spirituality and religion, making the essential point that spirituality is a gift bestowed on all human beings regardless of creed, class, color, or sexual orientation. Spirituality is recognizing that we have the power to change. We have the power to develop the healing process. Spirituality demonstrates that power. In my latest books, *The Angel and the Frog* and *The Happy Heretic,* I have quoted some key issues that bring this book current with some ideas I believe to be essential to living the spiritual life.

In this revised edition, I also have sought to relate spirituality to some of the key concerns facing recovering people today: relationships, relapse, and treatment issues. You do not need to be a philosopher, theologian, or student of history to understand the living challenge that spirituality offers, so I have sought to relate spirituality to contemporary and everyday situations. God is to be found in the ordinary.

I believe the all-embracing message that spirituality

1

brings is essential to the living of a positive lifestyle. It is too important to be missed. May you discover it now in the living of your life.

Leo Booth
Long Beach, California

Walking on Water

TO WALK ON WATER is to experience joy in living, to know the laugh and human embrace as well as the tear. Walking on water is seeing and feeling the given miracle of life in every moment. It is the shouted "yes" to all that life will bring.

Life is but a series of patterned moments, and with every moment comes decision. Which way shall I go? What shall I do? Shall I say yes or no? Our comfortableness with these decisions affect whether we live life or simply endure it.

Participate or spectate. Shape or wait. God gives us the gift of life and then invites us to create through it, with it, and in it.

In this sense, we are divine. In this sense, we are part of the divine drama. Every religion, creed, and culture gives this message, but few people listen. We miss the most important message in life: you are terrific.

We walk on water when we hear and accept this message.

The idea for this chapter comes from an incident that is recorded about Jesus and his disciples. In St. Matthew's gospel we read:

> After sending the people away, he went up a hill by himself to pray. When evening came, Jesus was there alone; and by this time the boat was far out in the lake, tossed about by the waves, because the wind was blowing against it.
>
> Between three and six o'clock in the morning, Jesus came to the disciples, walking on the water. When they saw him walking on the water, they were terrified. "It's a ghost!" they said, and screamed with fear.

Jesus spoke to them at once. "Courage!" he
said. "It is I. Don't be afraid!"

Then Peter spoke up. "Lord, if it is really
you, order me to come out on the water to
you."

"Come!" answered Jesus. So Peter got out of
the boat and started walking on the water to
Jesus. But when he noticed the strong wind,
he was afraid and started to sink down in
the water. "Save me, Lord!" he cried. (Matt.
14:23-31)

This incident tells more than Jesus doing supernatural
feats on a stormy sea, with Peter trying to imitate. The
miracle is in the words "take courage." Relative to the
physical and emotional needs of humankind, walking on
water means nothing. The incident only astounds and
amazes people. But the creative insight comes when we:

• absorb the revealed courage into our own lives

• take the courage that Peter reveals and relate it
  to our personal needs

- live away from those who have tried to rescue us from life

- face our challenges honestly

- realize an apparent failure as an opportunity for success

The miracle is discovered when we adapt the "take courage" into our own lives. We are the miracle. *We are terrific*.

Every area of life can reveal this truth: in personal relationships, music, religion, theater, politics, humor, craftsmanship, suffering, and poetry.

It is all out there, if only we have the eyes to see.

I recognized this when I was reading about the defection to the West of the famous ballet dancer Rudolf Nureyev.

On May 11, 1961, Rudolf Nureyev flew from Leningrad with the Kirov Ballet Company to dance in Paris. To the Russian authorities, Nureyev had already proven himself to be an individualist and a rebel. Not surprisingly, they had concerns about him even being in the

West. They sent a telegram to Paris, demanding that he return to Moscow, supposedly to perform before the Kremlin. Instead, Nureyev placed himself into the hands of the French police and asked for protection. Seizing the opportunity of the moment, he chose to defect. In the defection was courage: He chose to leave his family and country. He chose to leave the Kirov Ballet Company for . . . ? At the time, he did not know what.

The police took Nureyev and placed him in a solitary room. In Clive Barnes's book *Nureyev*, he quotes the dancer: "Then there was silence. I was alone. Four white walls and two doors. Two exits to two different lives."[1]

On that seemingly ordinary day in Le Bourget Airport in Paris, Rudolf Nureyev took courage and decided to shape his destiny. In the moment of defection, his remembered yesterdays generated a choice.

WALKING ON WATER

Nureyev affirmed, "For me this was already a return to dignity—the right to choose, the right I cherish most of all, that of self-determination."

The balanced life of spirituality is reached when we can comfortably hold together opposites: freedom and dependence; seeking God's will within the doing of our own; trusting and forever seeking God, yet exercising that divine gift of self-determination; holding together forces that often seem to point in opposite directions.

Paradoxes of God. Paradoxes of being human. Paradoxes of life.

It all begins to make sense when we accept that God wills for us real freedom. God created us to make choices. God created us to create. The dignity and nobility that all human beings can achieve is dependent upon this real freedom. In this gift is the miracle. We are human beings, not puppets on a string.

Our dependence upon God speaks of our creativeness. We did not create this universe. We are part of the miracle we call life. And yet part of the reality of this miracle is that we have the responsibility of decision. God's will for us is seeing our creative abilities and choosing to cooperate in positive living.

God is the continuous positive energy, the love for the world. God invites us to be involved. That makes us terrific!

To stand around and wait for God to make decisions in our lives is to miss the point, which is either apathy or cowardice or stupidity. God has already made a timeless decision. God wants what is best for us. God also wants us to want it.

The human paradox and confusion is revealed in these further remarks by Nureyev: "I did not have courage to stay here—just to come and stay. I did not have courage ... I remember I went to Church, I went to Mary ... and I said, 'Make it so that I stay without me doing it, you know, let it happen ... without me doing it ... that it will happen ... arrange so that I will stay.'"

We all know these feelings.

I know the fear of making a mistake or making the wrong decision. The desire to have others make the decision, others make the choice, others make it happen. Sometimes God.

I believe God makes good things happen in the world by putting deep within all of us the potential ingredients for creating the good life. As Genesis says in the creation account, "And it was good." We have the capacity for great goodness. The challenge of freedom comes in that we must want it too. The individual human being makes *goodness* demonstrable.

Jesus called Peter to walk on the water. Peter could have said no. The miracle of Peter walking on water is seen in the courage of his yes. As long as he had courage, it worked. When he began to doubt himself, he began to sink. The miracle for Peter was that for those few moments, he had divine courage. This is exactly what Nureyev did. He prayed for freedom. He wanted self-determination. He made a decision to defect for it. He left Russia, not because he wanted to dance, but because he wanted to dance *with freedom*. To dance is freedom. The miracle for Nureyev was that he knew what he wanted. He wanted it enough to risk everything. This is spirituality. This is walking on water.

What have these stories to do with spirituality? Everything. Spirituality is seeing all this fit together, seeing God in the confusions and decisions of life, seeing God in the never-ending doubts and fears, seeing God in the daily acts of often unnoticed acts of courage.

I want to explore a spirituality that includes everybody and everything, a spirituality that is connected with all aspects of living, and a spirituality that is the miracle of life, the magic of life, *mysterium tremendum* ("overwhelming mystery"), the divine event that makes our lives special.

Spirituality is creative living.

In *The Happy Heretic*, I asked: How did we become so spiritually dependent? How did we miss or ignore God's divine demonstration in our lives? Why would we want to minimize the power of choice in the living of our lives? How does it serve any religion to have millions of people pathetically dependent? What possible value is derived from such an extreme expression of religious codependency? The answer became obvious: *control*.

A New Message

Pelagius, a fourth century monk, proclaimed that there is a divine spirit, *spiritus*, the breath of God, in every human being, and this not only makes us special but also perfect.

Once his message is understood and accepted, then

everything changes. We are able to value the Scriptures for what they are rather than make them into something they were never intended to be. We appreciate religious ministers for what they say rather than elevate them onto pedestals beyond accountability. Also, we can respect other religions and philosophies, taking from them what will nurture and inspire our spiritual lives.

As I think about the power and fear that the church hierarchy used for hundreds of years to control millions of ordinary people, I'm suddenly aware of Rumi's poem "Blood Suckers from Hell." It suggests that the poetry that celebrates passion, freedom, dance, nature, and the humor of God makes the face of orthodoxy "squint like prunes."

Rumi speaking to a crowd muses:
"Watch out for those blood suckers from hell—'cause they're
    everywhere."
And the crowd wisely retorts: "That sounds serious—what
    do they look like, any hints; are they usually disguised?"
Rumi again: "Yes, usually, they are awful tricky!"
"How then to detect them?"

"Well,
I have noticed their eyes will narrow and their faces begin to
squint like prunes if they hear good poetry." [2]

Spirituality is experiencing our own personal power, experiencing the confidence of knowing we have the power to bring every good feeling into our lives, a power that is not paranoid or selfish. It is not cruel, prideful, or unworthy, but appreciates the abilities and individual gifts that we all have been given.

Spirituality is:

- the energy of adolescence and youth that constantly challenges, seeking new and often outrageous insights into living

- marriage and friendships that produce the qualities of love, tolerance, and loyalty

- artists working with wood or clay who continue the Genesis drama of creation

- musicians and songwriters reflecting the joys and sorrows of life

• maturity that encourages the young with the
  contribution of past experiences

In all the above is the spirituality of being human.
Nowhere is creative spirituality expressed more clearly
than in the gift of humor. The genius Albert Einstein was
once asked at a social gathering to explain his theory of
relativity.

> He said, "Madam, I was once walking in the
> country on a hot day with a *blind* friend, and
> remarked that I would like a drink of milk."
>
> "I understand drink," said my friend, "but
> what is milk?"
>
> "A white liquid," I replied.
>
> "I know liquid, but what is white?"
>
> "The same color as a swan's feathers."
>
> "I know feathers, but what is a swan?"
>
> "A bird with a crooked neck."
>
> "I know neck, but what is crooked?"
>
> I lost my patience, I seized his arm, and
> straightened it. Then I bent it at the elbow
> and said, "That is crooked."

"Ah," said my blind companion, "now I know
what you mean by milk."[3]

For those with eyes to see, spirituality is everywhere.
And it's okay to laugh.

Spirituality involves the journey into our real selves,
willingly wanting to face all that we will discover, the
good and the bad; the courage and the fear; the saint and
the sinner, realizing and accepting that what we discover
in ourselves will also be in others. That's life.

As the French writer Necondale said, "Human beings
cannot, while they live, be rid of life." Once we begin to
understand and accept these things, we have our fingers
on the power within the universe.

So long as we are in connection with life, we cannot
remove ourselves from life. I hope my book is helpful
to those millions of people who are suffering from the
disease of addiction, to those people in all parts of the
world who have addictive personalities and compulsive
behavior habits that make them want to seek escape from
their true selves.

In the everyday language of the drug addict, we see

the *great lie* exposed: The "getting spaced" experience is nothing less than a continued separation from reality and another way of feeling not good enough. The "trip" is nothing less than a journey away from who they are.

As a recovering alcoholic, I know the real feelings behind this language. I know what it is to search for meaning in a drug, to seek an answer in a drink, to crave happiness in a buzz. It is an escape from reality.

In my constant trying to please and satisfy, I lost me. In placing power out there, I became a slave. In struggling to make my insides match society's outsides, I did not fit.

Today, I meet people who acknowledge that they got high and were spaced on food, gambling, sex, and unhealthy emotional attachments.

They used *something* and progressively became lost, angry, afraid, and resentful.

Let the reader be the thermometer of his or her real needs.

A friend of mine asked, "Leo, are you implying that almost everyone is recovering from something? That society has become addictive?"

"Yes," I answered. "Look at the pain, loneliness, and

mindless violence, the obsessions with sex, food, money, people, not to mention alcohol and drugs. If the disease of addiction and obsession remains untreated, it will destroy our society."

The healing rests in the belief and confidence we have in ourselves. Do you believe that you can move mountains? Your belief is dependent upon seeing that such power is not located in the physical moving of mountains but in knowing that you were created to create.

The miracle is knowing in myself that I am walking on water when I am truly centered in myself. Knowing that I was created to live, that I belong to this world and the world belongs to me.

Wherever I am, that is where the center of the universe is. Wherever I am, that is where meaning has its beginning.

To know that I have a purpose in this world; to know in every fiber of my being that I am important and unique; to know that without me, the world would not be the same; to actually know that I make that much difference: This is walking on water.

To know that when the music is played or the song is

sung, you are involved and it lives through you. In a real way, you make what it is happen. In some mysterious and miraculous way, you are extending that creation within yourself and creating through it. It is emanating from you. Your being here makes the difference. To actually know this is to walk on water.

To know as you walk through the forest or up a mountain that in some real and unique way nature becomes a part of you and belongs to you; to know that anything that destroys and mutilates part of nature in some way destroys and mutilates you: This is to walk on water.

To know that the words we use are bridges of human contact, miracles of meaning by which ideas and feelings are expressed; to know that to stick rigidly and inflexibly to the word-meaning is often to miss reality and enslave the idea. If the Sabbath was made for humanity, so was the word. To take that word or phrase and shake it around, jump on it, kick it in the dust, and dress it in difference is the creation of something new and wonderful. This is what all great poets, writers, and artists do. They take the ordinary and make it extraordinary. They take the everyday and make it special. In the present, they reveal the future.

George Steiner said of Shakespeare, "Shakespeare at times seems to hear inside a word or phrase the echo of the future."

To know this is to walk on water.

Somewhere in this adventure and confusion is meaning; somewhere in this pain, tension, and death is meaning; somewhere in this mixed togetherness of fools, tyrants, and saints is meaning.

This is spirituality.

The blind man, when healed, still had to plant the seed and hoe the ground, wash his face and clean between his toes. Lazarus, after returning from the dead, still needed to discover the meaning of life. He still needed to pray for others and ask forgiveness. Perhaps these everyday aspects of living reveal the greater miracle.

Miracle is not found only in grand events. Great mystics and prophets need to eat, sleep, breathe, bathe, and listen to others. Miracle is found in the quiet place, the ordinary, the gentle word, and the welcoming smile.

We cannot walk on water unless we are prepared to risk, prepared to let go, take courage, and plunge into life.

Years after his defection, Rudolf Nureyev said in an

interview, "I am not one who is going to redo society, but I am going to show them where it is, which way to go. Reaching for something because reaching is something, rather than telling, for me is important."

This is spirituality. This is walking on water.

Miracle

EARLIER IN THIS BOOK, I talked briefly about Lazarus. He was the man whom Jesus brought back from the dead. It was a well-known miracle. Everybody knew about the raising of Lazarus. It still is popular among Christians.

It speaks of the power of God, resurrection, new life.

Lazarus had been dead for three days. St. John adds the insightful comment, "He stinketh" (John 11:39 KJV). After he had been raised from the dead and came out of his tomb, he was still bandaged in his burial clothes.

He answered Jesus's call. Interestingly, Jesus tells Lazarus's sisters to untie him and take care of him. Lazarus had not eaten anything for three days, the natural within the miracle, the supernatural wrapped in common sense. This kind of incident is what people expect miracles to be like: coming back from the dead; different; beyond belief; astonishing.

They expect a miracle to be something extraordinary, like moving mountains, making blind people see, or walking on water.

We experience something like this with David and Goliath. This story says something good about the little guy. I like this story. I am five feet seven inches tall!

The mighty Philistine army is fighting against Israel. The Philistines send out their warrior giant, Goliath. Israel is asked to do the same. Unfortunately, Israel has no one comparable in size. This is little David's big chance. David may be short in size, but he is big in confidence. David is chosen to represent Israel against Goliath.

Goliath started walking toward David again, and David ran quickly toward the Philistine battle line to fight him. He reached into his

bag and took out a stone, which he slung at
Goliath. It hit him on the forehead and broke
his skull, and Goliath fell face downward on
the ground. And so, without a sword, David
defeated and killed Goliath with a sling and
a stone! He ran to him, stood over him, *took
Goliath's sword out of its sheath, and cut
off his head and killed him*. (1 Sam. 17:48-51)

Goliath had complete body and head protection. He
carried a huge shield and long sword. He looked fierce.
He was tough. Only his face was left unprotected so that
he could see.

By contrast, David went into battle with a loose-fit-
ting tunic, carrying only a slingshot. He took five flat
stones. This was godly courage. Some people might call
it insanity!

The mighty colossus wielded his weapon. David felt
the breeze from the giant's swishing sword. He concen-
trated. He selected his stone, then slung it. A direct hit.
Goliath was struck in the temple. He fell. David chopped
off Goliath's head. Goliath is dead. A miracle.

Let me now describe a modern miracle. It concerns a

fat lady. Elizabeth, thirty-four, was suffering from obesity. She had suffered with an eating disorder for many years. She decided to go into the hospital for treatment. She slowly began to trust the staff at her therapy sessions. A doctor understood her. Counselors shared that they used to be like her. She saw the other patients struggling with honesty. She tried to be honest. She developed a love and respect for the hospital program.

It was not easy for her to trust others. She cried. At times she asked, "Why?" She remembered past painful incidents. Hurts were uncovered and discovered.

At times, Elizabeth felt scared. Was the treatment working? Was it a waste of time and money? Should she give up?

In spite of these doubts, she continued to trust. She experienced tough love, a day at a time. Her love and her trust grew. She began to listen. She began to hear.

She began to be able to take a compliment. Occasionally, she gave a compliment. She heard the messages from the counselors: "We love you. We see your pain. We hear you, hear your loneliness. We love you. At times the disease will say to you, 'You are no good. You don't deserve all this attention.' However, the healthy side of you wants to be loved. Needs the attention. Wants to share the pain and get better. The healthy side of you is the *real* you.

"Elizabeth, you are a miracle. Before the sickness began, you were God's miracle. God created you. You are God's miracle."

All these messages she heard. This in itself was a miracle. She heard compliments. She began to trust. After years of silence and hiding, she began to talk about her disease, about her pain, about being fat.

She explained her loneliness as a child. She talked about her father's drunken affection, his indelicate touch. She opened up more and talked about her mother's cold glance and constant criticism. The violence, the put-downs, the neglect, the isolation: Elizabeth put out all her pain.

Sometime during her childhood, Elizabeth learned how to eat. Eating brought satisfaction, comfort, and relief. She ate more to get more comfort. Enormous eating brought enormous satisfaction. She sneaked food. She hid food. Food became her protection from people, from pain, from criticism. Eventually, food took her on a *trip* away from her pain, away from reality.

Elizabeth spoke about her religious upbringing. It told her she was a sinner, a sinner needing repentance, needing salvation. She was a lost soul without Jesus, without the Holy Spirit, without the Bible. To enter heaven, she needed to be pure and obedient. She perceived her fears as guilt. Being human was being sinful; however, nothing was said about food. Sex was a sin; thinking sex was terrible. Nothing was said about food. Alcohol was a sin. Drugs were terrible. Nothing was said about food. It was okay to eat. Eating was good. And for Elizabeth, it felt good.

Elizabeth was a good eater. Her eating made her grandmother proud. Grandmother told Elizabeth that she was chubby and happy, that fat people are happy. Elizabeth wanted to please her grandmother, stay happy, and so she ate.

When Elizabeth visited friends, she learned how to please people. She ate all that was offered. All the cake. People smiled. She painfully remembered that one time when she said, "No more," everybody looked disappointed. Had she insulted the host? She felt guilt. She would never say "no more" again. She would never disappoint Grandmother or her friends again. She learned how to eat everything, then vomit afterward. Always in anger, guilt, loneliness, or fear, she would return to food. Even when her anger, guilt, and loneliness were caused by food, she would return to food. Everything revolved around food.

In the hospital, Elizabeth began to share this story. She wrote down her feelings and owned them. She saw her disease come alive in her written words. She discovered forgotten feelings—feelings she had swallowed with food, buried with the food, hidden in the food. Elizabeth faced her reality, then cried.

She came to see, understand, and accept the disease process. Her addiction was food. Like a drinking alcoholic, she would hide it, deny it, lie about it, lose her job because of it, get divorced for it, and suffer with it. Food was her mind-altering drug. Food worked; food brought satisfaction; food was instant escape. This is addiction.

Elizabeth's recovery and treatment began when she saw this, felt this, and accepted this. Elizabeth felt her pain, felt her addiction, and felt her disease.

Elizabeth was not a bad, crazy, ugly, or sinful woman. She was sick. She needed help. She had felt utterly alone. In the hospital, she met fellow sufferers, people who were being treated for the same disease. Their symptoms and pain were the same. And a growing number of people were demanding recognition for their disease.

The therapists introduced Elizabeth to the gentle art of loving herself. The treatment and recovery are for life.

Loving yourself begins when you feel your power, feel your freedom, feel your right to choose. This is spirituality.

Elizabeth did not choose the disease. She did not do anything to deserve it. She certainly did not ask for it; however, she has it. It is part of her. She can accept it, work on it, live with it a day at a time, or she can deny it and suffer. This is reality. The wrong choice gives power to the disease. The right choice keeps the power with Elizabeth. For Elizabeth to know this is to bring power, freedom, and miracle into her life.

The power and recovery rest in the feelings behind Elizabeth's eating. What is she eating? Is she eating on anger or guilt? Where is Elizabeth in her eating? If she is positive about her life, positive about her health, positive about her disease, she will choose the foods that love her, she will choose a balanced diet, and she will choose to eat to live rather than live to eat. Then she will experience good feelings that do not require food to feel good. She must practice abstinence, meaning a balanced and selected food program for continued recovery. Elizabeth must choose a style of eating that is good for her and choose meal plans that bring health.

For Elizabeth, the treatment was in giving her the knowledge to discover herself, the ability to share herself, to be the creative human being she was meant to be. Today, she has discovered the creative spirituality that comes with being real. Today, she is comfortable with herself. She is loved and loving in her new relationships. Confident in who she is, she is creating a new life, making her own world, and living in the solution, not the problem. She is accepting the support and program of Overeaters Anonymous. Oh, yes, and she is getting slimmer. Elizabeth is walking on water. Another miracle.

People can miss the miracle of Elizabeth because they have a narrow understanding of God's activity. They make miracle too exclusive.

Miracle is Lazarus, a man coming back from the dead. Miracle is Bartimaeus, a blind man seeing. Miracle is David killing the giant Goliath with a stone.

We make God too small; we make miracle too small; we make human beings too small. People are so busy looking for God, they miss God. God is in you and me.

Two men were talking in a bar. The atheist said, "There is no such thing as God."

The other man said, "Why do you say that?"

The atheist continued, "I asked God's help once when I was stuck in the desert, dying in the glaring sun. I cried out for God's help!"

The other man said, "Something must have happened. You are here now."

"Not really," said the atheist. "Some crazy Indian came and saved me!"

Traces of the Creator are in the created. We reflect the divine. In our action is the divine event. This is what the atheist missed.

So many people see miracles as God doing something to somebody, God working a miracle on somebody, or something out there brought down here. Miracle is seen as a divine intervention, like the parting of the Red Sea or the feeding of the five thousand. These events happen rarely. Today few people expect miracles.

I expect miracles and see them. The most common miracle is our ability to cooperate with the Divine. *We* can create. *We* can make miracles.

Instead of waiting for it, make it happen. Instead of waiting for God, demonstrate God. Instead of looking for a miracle, realize you are it.

At the end of *The Angel and the Frog*, I suggest that instead of waiting for an angel to come into our lives, we need to *become* that angel. "This is where it will begin," said Christine, the angel. "I know why I needed to be with you. And now *you* know. You were hoping for an angel to come and make everything okay. Well, you got your angel. He's a frog, or a hedgehog, or a cat, or a dog, or a mule, yes, one day, even a fox! Don't misunderstand me. I know I'm training to be an angel, one who brings a message, but the spiritual principles that lead to The Process are about discovering the message in the living of *our* lives."

"Will I see you again?" asked Cedric the frog.

"I will always be with you," said Christine. "When you really need me I will make my presence known and you will know it is me.

Now, join the other seekers and let the adventure begin."

Cedric closed his eyes and puckered his lips to give Christine a farewell kiss. He experienced a glow deep within him and then a cool breeze made its presence felt. He opened his eyes and Christine was gone.

People confuse miracle with magic. Magic is a trick, the pretended art of spells, charms, and rituals, done always to amaze, entertain, or control a group of people, an unreal experience that confounds us. Magic keeps the power with the magician or witch doctor or wizard. We, the people, are spectators. We make no contribution. We add nothing. We helplessly watch the magician's power and spells.

Many religious people, in ignorance, pray for magic. They want magic, ask for magic. This desire for magic was the backdrop to Jesus's desert temptations at the beginning of his ministry.

Jesus returned from the Jordan full of the

Holy Spirit, and was led by the Spirit into
the desert, where he was tempted by the Devil
for forty days. In all that time, he ate nothing, so that he was hungry when it was over.

The Devil said to him. "If you are God's
Son, order this stone to turn into bread."

But Jesus answered, "The scripture says,
'Human beings cannot live on bread alone.'"

Then the Devil took him up and showed him
in a second all the kingdoms of the world.
"I will give you all this power and all this
wealth," the Devil told him. "It has all been
handed over to me, and I can give it to anyone
I choose. All this will be yours, then, if you
worship me."

Jesus answered, "The scripture says, 'Worship the Lord your God and serve only him!'"

Then the Devil took him to Jerusalem and
set him on the highest point of the Temple,
and said to him, "If you are God's Son, throw
yourself down from here. For the scripture
says, 'God will order his angels to take good
care of you.' It also says, 'They will hold
you up with their hands so that not even your
feet will be hurt on the stones.'"

But Jesus answered, "The scripture says,
'Do not put the Lord your God to the test.'"
When the Devil finished tempting Jesus in
every way, he left him for a while. (Luke
4:1-13)

What kind of Messiah was Jesus going to be? Would he feed the poor by changing stones into bread? No! Would he offer circus spectacles from temple roofs? No! Jesus would offer no such mighty signs. No theatrics. No magic. Many religious people forget this message and seek the supernatural fix. They want God to work the trick in their lives, to take away the problems, to remove the sickness or disease, to stop the divorce, to get Alice through college, to keep George off the booze. "God, work your magic!"

God becomes the universal drug of choice. We get high on religion, take the Jesus trip, or say the prayer and the pain is gone. For a while, it seems to work. But it does not last. It is not real. Miracle requires cooperation. It demands something from us. It requires our investment. *Ask* and you shall receive. *Seek* and you shall find. *Knock* and the door will be opened. You must do something.

Let's go back to Lazarus. He answered Jesus's call in death as he had in life. He obeyed in death as he had obeyed in life. Jesus's desire to use him as a sign of life after death, a sign of the miracle within life, happened because Lazarus cooperated beyond the grave. I do not doubt the immensity of God's power working through Jesus, but Lazarus also had power. *If Jesus worked hard, so did Lazarus.* Remember, it was Lazarus who struggled in his burial bandages to walk. Then Jesus said to Lazarus's sister, "Untie him and let him go" (John 11:44).

In the bandages and the concern to untie him was the natural miracle. Had this been magic instead of miracle Jesus would have produced a dazzling Lazarus who would have danced out of the grave, humming a tune!

The miracle of David in the face of Goliath is his courage, determination, and skill as a marksman. David believed that God was with him and that God would spare Israel. David was prepared to fight for his beliefs. David made the miracle happen. He cooperated. He got involved.

Notice how David chose the weapon with which he was comfortable, the sling. King Saul wanted David to wear his armor and carry his kingly sword. David declined. Instead, he selected five flat stones and then stood his ground in the face of Goliath's taunts. David cooperated with God's will and produced the miracle. Magic would not have required a sling and flat stones. Magic would not have required human hunting skills. With magic, David would have puffed Goliath out of existence while peeling a grape!

My understanding of miracle always involves the human being. It requires cooperation and involvement. It is the exercise of human power, human freedom, and human choice.

This is what Elizabeth realized in treatment.

The miracle of life is discovered in life. People who get the most out of life are those who put the most into it.

The poet C. Day-Lewis said, "Earth is your talent. Use it." Do not wait for things to happen; make them happen. Those people who have made positive contributions to the world, inspired change, stimulated human understanding, and brought about the creation of justice all believed in themselves and their God-given power. They made things happen.

Martin Luther King Jr. had a dream and lived his dream. His dream involved human dignity for all people. Martin Luther King Jr. enabled others to dream. Where was the miracle? In his dream.

The same goes for Mahatma Ghandi. He worked for freedom. He worked for Indian dignity. He worked for lasting peace and justice. And he worked without using violence. Where was the miracle? It was in him.

And Mother Teresa epitomized the nobility of life and at the same time proclaimed the beauty of death. No child would die in her arms without love. Where was the miracle? It was in her.

Countless men and women from all races, religions, and creeds reveal the miracle of being human. What is the difference between them and you? Perhaps *you* forgot to believe in yourself. You forgot to believe in your miracle.

Remember the blind man in the gospel? He received the miracle of sight from Jesus, but he first had to shout for it. Many blind men were in Jerusalem, but Bartimaeus's difference came with the *shout*. He shouted his need so loudly that Jesus heard him. His shout produced the miracle. Probably people in the crowd told him to shut up, to be quiet. The blind man refused to listen. His people-pleasing days were over. Other blind and crippled people obeyed the crowd. But this blind man cried louder. They did not get it. He got it. Would he have received his sight had he not shouted?

Many lepers lived in Judea, and yet the lepers who were healed were those who walked for it. For miles, they walked on their crippled feet to find their healing. In the walking was the miracle. They walked, they asked, and they received.

What are you looking for in your life? What are your needs? The answers will be found within you. God created and is creating. When we are at our most positive, most receptive, most real, we are cooperating in God's will for us. We unite with God. We become *one*. These moments of miracle are constantly being offered to us, but we do not always realize it. We neglect our creative energy.

Have you ever stopped to consider how small we think? We get dulled by the machinery of life, and we miss the adventure, the fun, and the freedom. While I am writing,

I see the stars in the sky and I get in touch with belonging to something much bigger than my little world. The universe is incredible. The world is a mystery. And I am part of it.

Take the example of my Christian religion. I recently realized that the Mass is not just the Last Supper. It is not what the priest does with bread and wine. As Christians, we are not there simply to remember yesterday or worship a dead hero. The Mass is alive. It is the people. We, the people, do the Mass and make the sacrament. We meet as the body of Christ to share the body of Christ, to live as the body of Christ. Jesus did not live, die, and rise again for bread and wine. Jesus reflected God's power to the people. The Mass is the miracle of the people. Whatever absolution I receive must be lived out in the forgiveness I offer to others and myself. I am the Mass.

In the gift of life is the miracle given. God created the miracle in you and me, then he invites us to create. The wisdom comes in knowing that we have been given the power.

The following story explains where the power comes from.

A man dies and goes to heaven. He sees the door marked *God's Kingdom*, so he knocks.

God speaks from within. "Who is it?"

"It is I," the man replies.

"You cannot come in," God says.

I must be doing something wrong, thinks the man. Again he goes to the door marked *God's Kingdom* and knocks.

"Who is it?" God asks.

"It is I," the man says.

"You cannot come in," God says.

Finally, the man stops and thinks for a time. He smiles. He goes to the door and knocks again.

"Who is it?" God says.

"It is You."

"Come in," God says.

To know this is spirituality.

3

Spirituality

TWO FRIGHTENED LITTLE FISH were huddled together in the ocean, afraid to move. Out of the deep cave came a large beautiful fish with a glittering body. It was brimming over with confidence and began to pass the two little fish with great force. The big fish noticed their shivering forms, turned to them, and said, "Why stay huddled together? Why don't you swim out into the clear, glistening water?"

The two little fish looked at each other, and then one of them said, "Where is the water?"

This story highlights the problem facing many people. They are in life, and yet they are not living. You begin to live only when you recognize the spiritual power that has been given.

The little fish knew deep inside that they were missing something. They knew deep inside that they were not created to hide. They knew deep inside that the magic of life was escaping them, yet they wondered how to get it. Where was the water of life? The two little fish were huddled together, shaking with fear, not doing anything. Fear does this to people. Fear makes people frozen. Scared stiff. Petrified. Fear keeps people prisoners of themselves: the fear of rejection; the fear of not being understood; the fear of being considered too small, not good enough, not intelligent, or too plain, the wrong color, religion, and race: all of these fears group together to keep a person afraid and alone.

It is the difference between existing and living. Existing is what the two little fish were doing. Things happened around them, but they were unwilling to make things happen. They asked questions rather than delivered answers. The little fish never initiated anything.

They never did anything. They were prisoners of their frightened existence.

Many people are like this. For any number of reasons, they will not try new things, new experiences, and different happenings. They will not venture into new territories. The statement "I have never done that" becomes the mantra for never trying anything. This is the barrier that stops a person from experiencing new people, new ideas, new places, something different. Good experiences, like going to the theater, inviting friends for dinner, eating Chinese food, or visiting a foreign country, never happen because "I have never done that." It is the fear of the unknown.

This fear stops the experience of life, and it is self-imposed. It does not exist apart from ourselves. We create it and sustain it. We make our own fears and bring them into our lives. It is the bogeyman syndrome; the fears are products of our sick and frightened imaginations.

Life is not lived; it is endured. Fear of not being good enough stops you from being anything. Fear stops you from being somebody. Fear stops you from being yourself. We miss the joy of living by not taking risks. We miss the freedom experience, the people experience, the love experience, and the growth experience by waiting for life instead of seizing it.

How did we create this emptiness in our lives? By not saying hello to a passerby on our morning walk or jog. By not telling the family that we are afraid or lonely. By thinking that people are talking about us. Or by being afraid to speak in case the words come out wrong. John Donne said, "No man is an island." Yet many people feel they are isolated pieces of humanity. It is fear that creates this isolation.

Spirituality is the way out of this prison. It is the key that opens the door to yourself and to the exciting journey of life. When I give lectures about spirituality, people always ask, "How do I get it? How can I bring spirituality into my life? Is there a teach-yourself book?" These questions miss the essential point about spirituality. *Spirituality has already been given!* You and I have it. We are spiritual creatures, and the emphasis should not be on getting it or obtaining it but on *discovering it.* Life is to be experienced.

Spirituality is reality. I am aware of my spirituality when I am being real. Spirituality is my body, mind, emotions, and style—that essence of my being that makes sense to me and is essential to me. The more honest I can get, the more I understand and am understood. Of course, this honesty can be a frightening experience. When honesty is experienced, vulnerability is felt. Honesty is not just me sharing things, it is me sharing me. Also, the listeners, by their eyes and smiles, give me something of their lives. It makes for connection.

The more I share the real me, the more I can know the real you. In an honest conversation, I share and you bleed. Or you share and I bleed. The courageous part is the initial risk. Trusting. Letting go.

God sees our situations more clearly than we do, and to flow with God's creativity, we must be prepared to let go of old attitudes, ideas, people, and things. Life involves the risk of letting go. A story told at recovery meetings clearly affirms this:

Once upon a time, a man fell over a cliff. As he was falling, he reached out and grabbed at a branch. As he hung there, he shouted, "God, if you really do exist, please get me out of this mess!"

"This is God speaking. Please follow my directions carefully. One, let go of the tree," a voice said.

At this, the man shouted back, "Is there anyone else up there?"

God saw what the man could not see: a wide ledge a few feet below him. Let go and live.

Most times, we are not in contact with our God-given spirituality. We miss it, reject it, or ignore it. The time and occasions that we make contact, those wonderful occasions when we feel and touch the very essence of our life flow, we glow with enthusiasm. At such moments, it is great to be alive. It is not only great to be alive, it is great to be who we are and alive.

Such moments are abundant, but we often miss them. We concentrate on clutter, the superficial, the unreal, so that we miss the beauty that has been given and the splendor that surrounds us.

Are you in touch with your life? Are you there in your life? If you answer yes, then you are already aware of the thrill of living, the wonder of living, and that constant spirituality.

When two people are in love, it is loudly present. It shouts from their eyes, faces, and sprightly walk. Love is overflowing, demanding attention. It radiates from the most discreet, respectable, and proper people. It cannot be hidden or disguised. When two people are in love, life is filled with meaning and everything is exciting.

The shared telephone call between young lovers and the nervous pronunciation of the name sends shivers down the listening lover's spine. The meal and walk in the park become a sacramental communion that radiates a real presence. Even the making up after a silly argument becomes a joyous experience of generous forgiveness. Love makes everything exciting, meaningful, and extraordinary.

A young man who has been a prisoner of his homosexual feelings throughout his adolescence meets another man who says he feels the same. Yes, the other man actually says he feels the same way. He knows those hidden feelings. The young man is not alone. The other man says he wants to be a friend. Over a period of time, they become lovers. The experience is spiritual. The dirty touch is transformed into a caress of love. The pulsating bodily feelings that yesterday's religious men denounced as sinful are expressed in the healing sensation of mature sexuality. The love that dared not speak its name now has a confident message for a frightened people.

All over the world, different and separate minorities find hope in the risks a brave few are prepared to take. They find the courage to crawl out of their guilt-ridden prisons to breathe the free and fresh air of being who they are. Yes, the other man feels the same. That moment of spirituality is discovered in a new and different love.

The widower at the Senior Citizen's Club who finds in the widow Mabel a meaning and purpose in the latter days of his life is another whisper of this given love. Their comforting talk of how things used to be, the shared pride in their children, their doubled strength as they walk toward death are aspects of this spirituality. The sparkling, crinkled eyes of these two people tell the story that began yesterdays ago and will end in forever.

The Jewish family that adopts the Arab child; the young Yale graduate who offers three years' work in an underdeveloped country; the recovering alcoholic who visits prisons to tell his message of hope: all are whisperings of this loving life force. It is all around but rarely noticed. Yet look without and within, and it must be seen.

LET GO—LET GOD

It was the toys in *The Velveteen Rabbit* that found the secret to love:

"What is REAL?" asked the rabbit one day, when they were lying side-by-side near the nursery fender, before Nana came to tidy the room. "Does it mean having things that buzz inside you and a stick-out handle?"

"Real isn't how you are made," said the Skin Horse. "It's a thing that happens to you. When a child loves you for a long, long time, not just to play with, but really loves you, then you become REAL."

"Does it hurt?" asked the rabbit.

"Sometimes," said the Skin Horse, for he was always truthful. "When you are real, you don't mind being hurt."

"Does it happen all at once, like being wound up?" he asked, "or bit by bit?"

"It doesn't happen all at once," said the skin horse. "You become. It takes a long time. That's why it doesn't happen to people who break easily, or have sharp edges, or who have to be carefully kept. Generally by the time you are Real, most of your hair has

been loved off, and your eyes drop out, and
you get loose in the joints and very shabby.
But these things don't matter at all, because
once you are REAL, you can't be ugly, except
to people who don't understand."[4]

In every life, spirituality is to be discovered. We have
all had such moments. My definition for spirituality is
that which enables positive attitudes leading to creative
behaviors.

A wonderful and caring teacher at school told me that
God is against sin because it doesn't work! By sin, he
meant destructive and negative forces that corrupt what
is noble in humanity. History is full of tyrants and bullies
who achieved political power, and yet what they plotted
and killed for is no longer with us. Hate may be remembered, but it never inspires.

Spirituality is the essential remedy for all destructive
and negative attitudes because it produces positive and
creative lifestyles. Great lovers make great leaders.

If the little fish at the beginning of this chapter would
only love themselves, they would be swimming in the living waters. Spirituality makes the loving couple zealous

for life. It makes guilt-ridden gays positive and creative. It makes aged and crippled bodies gentle and hopeful.

These people are no longer preoccupied with what others think or say about them. They have accepted themselves. Instead of the prison of fear, they are in the flow of positive thinking.

The prison comes from having little love of ourselves. And when we feel or do things we were told not to feel or do, then we feel guilt and shame. To live in conformity, we learn how to block out reality, kill off the feelings, and act out a role. In blocking out the feelings, we block out our true selves. Soon, little is left. When asked how we feel, we look vacant. We are vacant. We are living another person's story.

Thousands are still taught how to play games and please people rather than be real. Even today, many people live a lie and exist to please. The creative and positive spirituality that is given by God at birth is atrophied by guilt and fear. Life is now exchanged for existence. Sickly prisons are built, and the tragedy is that most people are unaware they not only live in them but helped create them.

Some of these prisons were erected under the influence of over-enthusiastic and sick religious fanatics. Religious fundamentalists press guilt buttons, unexplained and misinterpreted Bible passages are used to condemn and control a variety of people, personal power is exchanged for religious codependency. Few people have heard the phrase *religious codependency*, and yet it is prevalent in every religion. It is the opposite of spiritual co-creation, working with God to create success. In *The Happy Heretic*, I explain religious codependency:

Most religious people are taught that they are completely dependent upon God for all of their wants and needs. Saint Augustine went so far as to suggest that we can do nothing good except through God's grace.

This message became a central dogma in the church and it affected everyone. The power of the church influenced most parts of the then-known world. Even non-Christians came to believe that they were sinful, inadequate, damaged, and completely dependent upon God.

Pelagius felt uncomfortable with this teaching because he said that it lacked balance. It affirmed only what God is doing; it didn't speak to our involvement. Don't we have a say in our lives? Where is free will? Where is choice?

"Suppose that I want to bend my finger or to move my hand, to sit, to stand, to walk, to run to and fro, to spit or to blow my nose, to perform the offices of nature; must the help of God be always indispensable to me?" (Coelestius, a disciple of Pelagius).

Becoming Creative

Pelagius realized that he was swimming against the tide of church tradition; everything in church worship spoke about what God was doing in His world. And from this worship and religious instruction developed messages that we have all heard at one time or another:

• If God wants you to have it, then it will happen.

• There, but for the grace of God, go I.

• When your time is up, God will take you home.

• What God has joined together, let no man put asunder.

In *The Happy Heretic*, we consider what our part is in the above messages; we discover what is to be found in the other hand. Let's examine them:

If God wants you to have it, then it will happen.

I do not believe that we have a job, wife, car, or a college degree because God wanted us to have them; *I'm convinced that we also did something*. We attended the interview with an excellent resume, we got to know and love the woman who is now our wife, we saved for the car that we now own, and yes, we studied hard for our exams.

There, but for the grace of God, go I.

I always liked this saying until I began to think about it. Do I really want to suggest that we are in prison or homeless because God's grace stopped these tragedies from happening to us? Should we thank God that we're not like those we feel sorry for, or do we need to feel good about the circumstances, actions, or choices we've made that prevented us from going to prison or not being able to make our house payments? Our *choices* create success in life and we are necessarily involved, even if we're not always conscious of it.

When your time is up, God will take you home.

This saying feels appropriate when we die at eighty in a comfortable bed with family around us, but it is not so acceptable when our teenage sons or daughters are killed by a drunk driver, or they die as a young soldier in a war. Does this comment seriously suggest that God directed the drunk driver or created the war?

What God has joined together, let no man put asunder.

In any marriage, healthy or unhealthy, both people are involved. The choice to marry is made for many reasons, and sometimes one or both people hold unrealistic expectations; however, *it is the two people who make their marriage work*. Yes, God is involved, but He does not magically keep the couple together.

It is also unacceptable, especially if abuse is involved, to invoke a promise made before God to keep a toxic relationship together.

God's Grace Abounds

I believe that God is involved in everything and, using traditional language, His grace abounds; however, we play an essential role in the living of our lives.

We are able to live the good life when we know, on a spiritual level, that we make life come alive. Our decisions and choices determine success or tragedy. God doesn't *make* anyone happy, sad, successful, or loving . . . that's our job.

All religions are institutions built by men who speak for God. Most religions have a power structure that involves creeds, holy writings, dogmas, priests, ministers, food laws, rules and regulations, an objective morality, and social customs that have evolved from various ethnic traditions. Some religions, to their credit, have willingly accepted the customs of other cultures and developed in unity.

All religions are essentially earthbound, seeking to teach us how to live the good life, claiming the occasional divine intervention. Herein lies the dilemma: What is true? Is it all true because the Bible and tradition say so, or do we need an intelligent and sensitive interpretation?

It can be clearly demonstrated that many of yesterday's dogmas have today been downplayed after the development of science and modern medicine. A study of religion often tells us more about the people who believe than the spiritual qualities they believe in.

All religions have rules and teachings that encourage heavenly thoughts and aspirations, but also produce earthly prejudices and resentments. The Protestant and Catholic antagonism is a variation on the Arab and Jewish conflict, which can be compared with the Muslim and Hindu disagreements. Whatever ingredients are added to the religious cake, for the majority of the people, it seems to be a gastronomical mess. My advice is that spiritual people are wise to be on a severe religious diet!

An understanding of religion that I share is expressed by a Hindu teacher, the late Baba Maktanada, who had an Ashram in Oakland, California. He said:

> Every religion is okay in its own right.
> There may be religions—not hundreds, but thou-
> sands of religions. Yet, how many Gods are
> there to bestow their grace upon all these
> religious people? God in one, He can't become

two. Does God belong to the Hindus? Is He a Christian? Is He Jewish? Is He a Sufi? Does He belong to Buddhism? Is He Black? Is He White? Is He Red? To whom does He belong? These are important questions and worth contemplating.

Now it is very likely that because He is God, He belongs to everybody. For Hindus, He is Ram, and for Christians, He is called God. For Sufi, He is Allah, and for Zoroastrians, He is Zarathustra. Everyone calls Him by a different name.

After pursuing all these religions, we should learn how to cultivate the awareness of Universal Brotherhood. Don't pursue these religions so that we can murder one another with distinctions. All countries belong to Him, all languages belong to Him, all mantras belong to Him, and all religions belong to Him. He belongs to everybody. All the people who follow different religions should attain this understanding.[5]

This reveals a spiritual understanding of religion. Spirituality is given. It is what it is to be a human being. It is that given spark of creativity, yesterday's soul. Words change, but the gift remains. It is that which is real about the human being. It is the essential personality, both different and unique. You can live without religion, but you only exist without the awareness of spirituality.

How do you get in touch with your spirituality? It is the responsibility of every individual to seek, discover, and nurture their own. You are responsible for you. You are responsible for the joys and chaos you choose to make. You are responsible for your life.

And that takes us close to the problem: many people will not accept responsibility for themselves. We complain, we get angry, we harbor resentments, and do not see that we are bringing the pain into our lives and attaching ourselves to the pain.

My existence stems from where I am. Whether I choose to write a book, go to work, or even consider it a good day is dependent upon my attitude. To miss this is to miss me. Miss my life.

The good morning remark in the park or the evening embrace before sleep reflects our attitude as individuals. How we speak to others affects our developing spirituality. Because I believe it is God's world and we demonstrate God as a people, I know that it is my world and your world. We are collectively responsible for our world.

Also, the kind word can be said only if we choose to say it. That needed word of encouragement or forgiveness requires you. Others may say it, but that would not be you. It would not be you saying it. Remember, nobody can say it like you can. You are terrific. In your individuality is your uniqueness. In your individuality is your power. In your individuality is God expressed.

Everything stems from how we choose to practice our spirituality. The word of encouragement or the silence of understanding: All are part of life. All are our responsibility. Even the negative and critical statements are ours. We choose to hurt. We choose to be cruel. We choose to destroy. The awareness of our imperfections can be the way back to our given spirituality. Jesus explained this attitude to life in the story about the priest and the sinner:

> He also spoke this parable to some who trusted in themselves that they were righteous, and despised others: "Two men went up into the temple to pray, one a Pharisee and

the other a tax collector. The Pharisee stood
and prayed thus with himself: 'God, I thank
You that I am not like other men, extortion-
ers, unjust, adulterers, or even like this
tax collector. I fast twice a week; I give
tithes of all that I get.' And the tax collector, standing afar off, would not so much
as raise his eyes to heaven, but beat his
breast, saying, 'God, be merciful to me, a
sinner!' I tell you, this man went down to his
house justified rather than the other; for
everyone who exalts himself will be humbled,
but he who humbles himself will be exalted."
(Luke 18:9-14 NKJV)

Let me explain. I am an alcoholic. I do not know why I
am alcoholic. Nobody in my immediate family is alcoholic.
It is not something I ever seriously intended to be. Whether
the disease is biological, psychological, or environmental
seems interesting only for after dinner conversation. Such
talk is redundant to my survival. The important fact is that
I have the disease, allergy, sickness of alcoholism, and it is
essential that I accept it and live with it.

In simple terms, I cannot drink alcohol and get away

with it. I have problems when I drink alcohol.

In real terms, alcohol was the way I avoided living with me. History teaches me this. My history of my drinking teaches me this.

I now know and accept what I am. I am an alcoholic. Yesterday's games only hurt me and those who loved me. In my years of denial, when I claimed that I had fooled psychiatrists and bishops, I now see that I only fooled me.

Now I see. I am the only thing I have. When I have me, I have everything. Without me, I have nothing. I believe today that it would be insane to neglect, hurt, or destroy the me—I mean all of me—that I have to work with: This is me.

It is good for family and friends to accept that I am alcoholic, but it is essential for me to know and accept it. I not only live with it, but accept the reality of this disease. I bring my alcoholism and my recovery into the living of my life. I make the disease work for me and use the disease in my life to live. The young couple in love used their relationship to experience a spiritual communion. The widower and Mabel used their loving companionship to face death. Well, the acceptance of my disease brings spiritual growth into my life.

I believe that spirituality is given. It permeates the fabric of being human. The more I can discover about myself, the more love I can give myself, and this will involve loving and accepting my alcoholism. That is spirituality.

I tried to drink alcohol like other people and I ended up drinking alcohol like a drunk. I was never ordinary or balanced in my drinking. When I did manage to control my drinking at a dinner party, I always wanted more. Now I know that the problem was not the alcohol but the person drinking the alcohol. The drinking was the symptom of the sickness, but the real disease lived in my loneliness, guilt, feelings of isolation, anger, and personalized pain.

All these painful feelings were me. I hid the sickness behind a face of confidence and crazy merriment. Drinking only enabled me to escape to Fantasy Island and live the fantasy; and this escape was painful.

I always wanted to be like other people. I wanted my insides to match other people's outsides. I wanted to experience what you looked like. I wanted desperately to be loved and accepted by you. I would do anything, be anything, say anything to please you. I was living my life for you. I felt that without you, there was no me.

I was not tall enough. My brain was not good enough. My family was not rich enough. I never wanted you to discover what I really felt or thought about me, so I hid them and buried them deep within me. By being permanently on stage, I could keep the world out of my tragic life. I would let you see only what I wanted you to see.

Long before alcohol, I hid behind pretensions and lies. I could play games and weave webs that kept everybody who was concerned going in circles. Alcohol only added to the confusion, occasionally making me feel good. I drank myself into courage, elegance, and brilliance. I was the next best thing to God. At times, I was God.

The disease progressed and I was taken deeper into the world of fantasy. Alcohol deceptively was taking me away from the uncomfortable world I had lived in for such a long time. When I experienced pain or problems, I reached for my friend in the bottle. In a few gulps, I could exchange reality for fantasy. For the price of a bottle of gin, I could create my own world and keep the real world out. Alcohol was my fix. Alcohol was my drug of choice.

Some people use food, others use drugs and pills. Some get high on power and sexual conquests. Thousands play one drug against another; they mix up the compulsions. The drug may vary, but the reason is the same: *escape*. The disease is the same for all of these compulsions; it is preferring fantasy to a life in reality. The loneliness, isolation, and fear of people is more telling about alcoholism than wet beds, car crashes, and midnight brawls.

You can remove the alcohol from my alcoholic system, brain, and lifestyle, but you cannot remove the alcohol-*ic*. It is the *ic* that wants me to drink again, escape again, people please again, hand over my power again, run from and into pain again. The *ic* is that sick part of me that I need to take care of, be responsible for, and seek to manage. The only hook the *ic* needs to run rampant in my life is the desire to be unreal, the wish for fantasy, the urge to escape, the little white lie that supposedly nobody cares about. Once you indicate that you want out of your life, the *ic* wants in.

Notice I have not mentioned being drunk. You do not need to drink to experience the insanity of a drunk. The alcoholic can still be suffering from the disease of alcoholism without having a *physical* drink. The temper tantrums, deceits, ego trips, aspects of denial, seeking to control and take charge of the lives of others, unresolved anger, and resentments: all of these are symptoms of the dry drunk. Spirituality is not an interesting option for the addict; it is *essential*. It is the essence of his program for sobriety and peace of mind. A realized spirituality is daily recovery.

In the clear vision of surrender, the latent stirrings of recovery and success can be seen. The bridge of trust between human beings is the disclosure of actions and attitudes we most dislike. In the open discussion of our darker sides is the seed of acceptance sown.

For many people, spiritual growth comes with the acceptance of a disease, the acceptance of something that will destroy them if left untreated, and the acceptance of addiction. This is the moment that births a powerful and living spirituality. A. Alvarez wrote in *The Shaping Spirit*, "There is a moment at which things come truly alive; the moment at which they are caught in all their subtlety by the imagination. They then take to themselves meaning."[6]

Sharing is such a moment. My need to share, my need

to tell you how I feel, my need to reveal my wounds with you keeps alive the reality of who I am. To let go of my resentments and destructive attitudes is the beginning of freedom. To let go and let God is to discover this given spirituality.

Here is a powerful poem that explores the concept of letting go; it was written by a woman in prison:

After a while you learn the subtle difference between holding
  a hand and chaining a soul.
And you learn that love doesn't mean leaning and company
  doesn't mean security.
And you begin to learn that kisses are never contracts and
  presents aren't promises.
And you begin to accept your defeats with your head up and
  your eyes looking ahead, with the grace of a woman not
  the grief of a child.
And you learn to build all your roads on today, because
  tomorrow's ground is too uncertain for plans.
Futures have a way of falling down mid-flight.
After a while, you learn that even sunshine burns if you ask
  too much. So you plant your own garden and decorate

*your own soul, instead of waiting for someone to bring
you flowers.*
*And you learn that you really can endure, that you really are
strong.*
And you really do have worth. And you learn and you learn.
With every good-bye you learn . . .

4

My Moment

THERE ARE TIMES, I call them moments, when you are given the opportunity to see and understand who you really are. The one special moment I wish to describe occurred after my last drunken car crash. I left the bar at 3 PM and almost made it home. I was seconds from my home in England when I crashed my car and was almost killed. That catastrophe became an opportunity to experience something I needed to know. From the debris of a car crash, I had a moment of sanity, a moment when I could see something, a moment when I could know something and I could grow. I came in touch with the real me.

I had a glimpse of the real Leo. I am not saying this was the first time I was aware of being drunk; that was a common experience! The miracle of this moment was that it was the first time I was aware of having a serious alcoholic problem. I became aware that I was sick, aware that I was alcoholic. A moment of suffering became an opportunity for growth and joy. What I share in this book has its roots in that happening years ago.

In that special moment after the car crash, I saw my alcoholic fantasy, my insane drama, my erratic impulses, and my absolute loneliness and utter isolation. I emerged from the crash realizing something I had denied for years: I was an alcoholic. Let me say that again and bring it into today. I *am* an alcoholic.

Amid the shouts and screams from women with perambulators, motorists trying to redirect cars around smoldering metal, mumblings from a growing audience staring at a drunken priest with his head between his knees at the side of the road, a part of me was saying:

You know you really are an alcoholic.

Problems happen when you drink.
Your drinking will ruin your life and destroy you.
What are you going to do?

But the most constant theme in my mind's group committee meeting was: "You are an alcoholic."

I am not saying that I completely surrendered or that I fully accepted or understood the implications of my alcoholism. I was no St. Paul on the Damascus Road with a voice from Jesus halting me in my tracks. Oh, no! I heard no voices from the beyond. These voices came from within:

You are an alcoholic.

While all this was happening, I experienced the uncanny feeling of standing outside of myself, seeing the confusion and the horror with startling clarity, and looking at me, drunk, with my head between my legs. From above the smoke and noise, I stared at me. I had never seen me quite like this before. Oh, yes, I had often caught myself drunk, caught myself in the act of drunken rage or vicious sarcasm, and I had even stopped myself from banging doors or smashing china, but I had never seen me like I was seeing me now.

I knew that the drunk at the side of the road was not the real me. I knew that the priest who loved his work, loved God's world, and loved people was within the same man being comforted at the site of the car crash.

I knew that the real Leo was inside that sick and inebriated person and that now was the time for him to begin to come out. I experienced the spiritual through the pain. The moment of seeing was now. The moment of healing could begin. The moment of miracle was given.

This moment was crucial to my recovery, crucial to my understanding of the disease, and crucial to my thinking about treatment. For years, people had said that I drank too much. For years, people had tried to make me see, make me understand, and make me face up to myself. They tried to force me into accepting my sickness, my allergy, and my disease. On most occasions, I would mouth verbal abuse or implausible excuses. But now I was seeing it, seeing me.

And instantly, I moved from seeing to saying: I am an alcoholic.

I was admitting to myself that I was an alcoholic. For me, that was, and still is, a cherished miracle.

In England, we have the phrases "The penny dropped" and "The ice broke," which are used to describe moments when the truth collides with life, and the human being is given a personal and undeniable insight into reality.

For the first time, you actually know. I mean, know, really *know*! I had looked many times, but now I was seeing. I had listened many times, but now I was hearing. I reached a point of awareness, and I was involved with reality. It is frightening. It is tremendous. It is real. When I saw and tasted my disease, I experienced the beginning of my recovery. In the facing up, in the confrontation, in the encounter with the disease, I grasped the possibility of my recovery.

When I read I Corinthians, it speaks to my moment of awareness. "When I was a child, my speech, feelings, and thinking were all those of a child. Now that I am an adult, I have no more use for childish ways. What we see now is like a dim image in a mirror; then we shall see face-to-face. What I know now is only partial; then it will be complete, as complete as God's knowledge of me" (1 Cor. 13:11).

In this passage, I am made to see that I can change. *You are an alcoholic. Leo, you are an alcoholic,* so said the voices within. I agreed.

As I write these words, I feel the past emotions welling up to the surface. I am so grateful. I know something about me, something true, something real, something as descriptive as the color of my eyes. This I needed to know.

I made a discovery that enabled me to open the door to a new life. From the car crash, I discovered something about me. I now had an awareness of me that was real. I had a cherished moment when I said what I secretly knew: "I am an alcoholic."

In that moment, I realized something spiritual.

I perceived and discovered given spirituality.

It is like knowing the feelings of love. When two people are in love, they have strong feelings for each other: excitement, anxiety, joy, vulnerability, and need. In such emotions, the real self is experienced. You are in touch with the real you. You know something about yourself. Love is spiritual because it is true. It makes you feel. Love makes you more real.

Another example might be seen in the child who has struggled with a geometry problem for days, and then inexplicably, everything fits into place. You reach a moment of clarity. You see beyond the equations. The answer screams at you. You solve a problem when you see the problem in its entirety. The solution is in the problem. The recovery is in the pain. Such is the moment.

Another insight might be seen in the biblical statement at the beginning of Genesis:

> Then God commanded, "Let the water below the sky come together in one place, so that the land will appear"—and it was done. He named the land "Earth," and the water which had come together He named "Sea." And God was pleased with what He saw. Then He commanded: "Let the earth produce all kinds of plants, those that bear grain and those that bear fruit"—and it was done.
>
> So the earth produced all kinds of plants, and God was pleased with what He saw. (Gen. 1:9–12)

These wonderful words take on meaning and become

real only when we see the beauty of nature and experience the green trees, rippling streams, and warm winds. God's beauty is recognized in creation. God is seen in the mountains and the forest. In the awesome power and mysterious depths of the ocean is God's majesty perceived. God's portrait is in God's creation, our world.

We must feel through these inadequate words to an understanding; words are but the bridges toward reality.

In the energetic birth of a human being eager for life, God's creativity is seen. The baby's first cry is nature's resounding yes to God. We must see God in the given, in the flesh and blood of life, in the beauty and energy of nature.

God's moments are many and various, yet so often we miss them. We miss them because we miss ourselves. So long as we persist in seeking God out there, we will miss the miracle of the given: the miracle of the ordinary; the bald man sharing his lunch with the sparrow; the mother duck teaching the ducklings to swim; the thrill of jogging in the rain. These are the given miracles of life.

My moment after the car crash was a miracle because it put me in touch with who I am. It enabled me to see something I needed to see. Needed to know. It took me deeper into myself. The place where I must live. This is true not only for the alcoholic, but for everybody. Life, experiencing life, feeling life are the contact points that enable us to discover who we are. In the understanding of my history is my future.

Everyone has moments when the writing is on the wall. We see it in our lives. We ignore it at our peril.

Incidentally, I am sure that I had other moments before the car crash that revealed my alcoholism: my disease, my compulsive and obsessive behavior, but I either denied or ignored them. I was not ready to receive it.

The God of truth created a world of moments, but our part is to be willing to see them. God is the continuous moment, but I have to want it, see it, grasp it.

I have to willingly want my recovery. In this sense, *truth is personal.*

God did not try to reach me that day more than any other day. God did not think: "Let's force Leo into acceptance. Let's make a horrid car crash for Leo when he is drunk." Such a God would be in need of treatment!

God was always loving me, even in my worst moments.

Whether I am a vomiting drunk or a recovering priest, God's love is the same. God's love is constant for all creatures. God loves. Period.

It is not a case of a temperamental God loving more or less on any given day. Still less is God's love proportionate to our success; rather, it was that I cooperated with God's will for me when I made a move toward my recovery. I made a move to help me. I began the slow process of loving me back to health. I created the moments by responding to the moment.

Not only did I respond at the time of the car crash, but to this day, I have chosen to keep that moment alive. When I choose to remember my last drunk, I respond to God's constant love responsibly. I continue to cooperate with the miracle. I keep the miracle alive. I make the miracle happen today. I keep the moment alive.

To quote the famous Christian mystic Simone Weil, "Our consent is necessary in order that God may perceive His own creation through us." The alcoholic's disease is not the alcohol. The drug addict's problem is not in the syringe. The overeater's compulsion does not exist in the fridge. Las Vegas is not the real enemy of the gambler. The disease of addiction and obsession lives within the human being. The disease hides in our feelings and emotions of utter isolation.

Those who are aware of the symptoms of the disease in their own lives, those who are recovering a day at a time, those who by marriage or having been born into an alcoholic family, those who are in a relationship with the disease and have a program of recovery, such people are capable of understanding and giving helpful advice. From their personal experiences, they see the disease's cunning and baffling characteristics. And they can confront it.

MY MOMENT

Those alcoholics who have only recently discovered that they have the disease are wise to listen to those who have been clean and sober for some years. It is common sense to seek the support of those who are sober, those who are living comfortably and serenely a day at a time with the disease. I realize that nobody is the same, and everybody's life has different aspects and characteristics, but the diseases of alcoholism and addiction have identifiably common symptoms. Just as the various strains of flu have common symptoms that require the same treatment for the British in London and the Filipinos in Manila, so the symptoms for alcoholics, drug addiction, and compulsive eating or gambling are identifiable (generally speaking) to all sufferers.

Incidentally, recovery also has identifiable characteristics. It is not sensible to arrogantly go your own way when it is alarmingly different from the experience of the recovering community around you. I have described how the moment of my accepting the disease was and is tremendously important for my growth as a person; however, that growth has been sustained within the recovering community. In the common sharing about

my disease with recovering people, I am able to use yesterday's horror stories to recharge a positive and creative
lifestyle today. Listening to how other people have grown
and live with their alcoholism helps me live with mine.
This is true not only for the alcoholic, but for all who live
with a compulsive and obsessive disease.

The moment the person with an eating disorder is
willing to accept that they have a disease and need help is
the moment when healing and recovery can begin. The
disease should not be seen in the food, but in the destructive attitudes and behaviors that are at work in the person's life. We can discuss our true feelings only when we
feel it is safe to own our feelings, okay to say who we are,
and safe to say what we feel. Remember, the disease of
compulsion and obsession feeds on fear, loneliness, anger,
hatred, denial, guilt, and self-pity.

We deny ourselves any creative and balanced pleasure
for an indulgence in food that makes us feel sick, sad, and
guilty. Then we vomit; we purge ourselves. The vicious
cycle is triggered. We feel self-pity and bad because we
eat, and yet our disease tells us that the only comfort and
satisfaction we get in life comes from eating. We eat on

anger, depression, lack of sex, loneliness, fear, or isolation. The key to recovery is spirituality. Spirituality is in seeing, appreciating, and recognizing the beauty that exists within and the power to change.

We must love beyond the fatness into our real selves. We must force the honesty through the layers of flesh to realize and appreciate the beautiful person within. If we have a poor opinion of ourselves, if we do not think we are of much value, if we are unable to see any positive features in our lives, it is not surprising that we continue to destroy ourselves.

Help comes when the individual hears his or her own cry. Recovery is available if the person really wants it, is prepared to ask for it, and will work for it. Using the analogy of the drowning man, unless he shouts, he cannot be rescued. Unless he lets go of the rock that is pulling him down, he will not survive; however, he must make the first move. He must let go.

People who have problems with drugs, alcohol, gambling, food, or any situation that is out of control will be able to identify with the above feelings, and for recovery to begin, the person concerned must make the first move.

I do not mean that we cannot get help from other people or self-help groups, but nobody can help until we make some kind of positive response to our pain. That is why the moment is so important. Having reached that point in our lives when we can see and hear the truth, I mean really see, really hear, and really understand what is happening in our lives, this becomes the moment of change. When we perceive that the disease of unmanageability and powerlessness exists within our personal lives, when we see that we need to take responsibility for the disease that is destroying us, we begin the moment of recovery.

As with all diseases, the symptoms are clear to those with eyes to see and ears to hear. The symptoms need to be shouted out for the sufferers to hear. It is often therapeutically beneficial to get the sufferers, the patients, to shout out their symptoms, to shout them out so that the experience brings its own personal perceptions. I deliberately use the word *shout* because that point of urgency and pain must be reached before sufferers can hear their need.

In the screamed shout are the symptoms expressed:

fear, loneliness, depression, anger, resentments, apathy, tiredness, confusion, insanity, faithlessness, hatred, rage, sadness, aggression, impotence, annoyance, broken relationships, physical violence, unemployment, poor physical health, low self-esteem, police convictions, treatment in a mental hospital, and suicide attempts. The life of an addict is a life of torments, a self-inflicted personal torture chamber.

It is like the victim giving sticks to the mugger, cringing and crying, "Hit me." Until the sufferer sees this insanity, the disease will always win. Rigorous honesty, removing the mask of hypocrisy, and seeing the lies and manipulations that feed the compulsive and obsessive behavior is the treatment that must become the life we call recovery.

Many who have gone through treatment call their life a program, a daily spiritual orientation, or an altered lifestyle. The disease is arrested by the honest decision you choose to make concerning your life. Deciding to be honest, to experience the now, to live a day at a time, to admit when in the wrong is to live the spiritual life.

When I begin to love myself, I begin to love God and God's world. When I hate myself, I miss God and God's world. Knowledge becomes a healing force: "Physician, heal thyself" (Luke 4:23 KJV). Yes, God is involved in your treatment, but so are you. Your cooperation is divine. That part of God that is you must be involved in recovery.

The discovery of who you are, including your wound-edness, is spiritual. It is positive and creative, and with it we build bridges to other human beings in need. In the shared suffering of the recovering addict with the suffering addict is the miracle of healing given.

This great adventure turns out to be the only adventure worth taking for any human being—the journey into self.

So I return to that crazy journey that led to the car crash. You remember, I did not make it home. Now I can see that it was impossible for me to ever arrive home by going that route. Even if I had parked the car in the garage, entered the house and closed the door for the night, clumsily undressed and got into bed, I still would have been a long way from home. The birth of my disease began with the journey away from me, fed, encouraged, and supported by my alcoholic drinking, my addiction.

That place in me that prefers fantasy to reality is where my disease lives. For years, it was camouflaged and hidden by my low self-esteem and feelings of guilt. The alcohol took me further and further away from me, and at the time of my car crash, I was a long way from home. I was years away from where I was meant to be. The car crash made this clear. I saw what was happening to my life. This is why that moment is so special and important to me today. It proved to be the point at which I started to go home to me.

When I saw the film *E.T.*, I saw my life and my addiction more clearly. Like E.T., I had accidentally entered the wrong world, and I could not survive in that world. The drinking world was not where I was meant to be. I was not physically equipped to drink alcohol. E.T. needed to go home to live. I needed to go home to the reality of my alcoholism to survive. To be comfortable in my world, I needed reality. The choice was mine. Choice is part of my story. It still is.

The young boy in *E.T.* also had a choice. Would he stay home with his family or go to another world with E.T.? He chose to stay in his real world.

I needed to make a choice to discover the real me. Saying I was an alcoholic was just the beginning; I must now live with my choice, live with my disease.

Life is a series of moments. All are special, but some stand out. I thank God for the moment I knew what for years others had said: "I am an alcoholic." I am glad I know it. I do not like my alcoholism, but I have grown to love it, because it is an essential part of who I am. What about you?

Two Heads

HISTORICALLY, HUMANS HAVE OFTEN seen themselves in the middle of a supernatural battle: the forces of light against the forces of darkness; evil trying to destroy truth; Satan seeking power in God's world.

Sacred books recount it. Religions immortalize it. Dante's *Inferno* endeavors to describe it. It is not just a biblical theme. People today are still preoccupied with it. Superman stands for truth against the various gangsters of terror. Batman and Robin encounter every danger to stop the dastardly deeds of the pernicious Penguin.

Nowhere is this seen more clearly than in the epic drama of *Star Wars*. In the saga, a small but noble army of Jedi fight the terrifying legions of the Empire led by the ex-Jedi, Darth Vader.

Such dramas feed our imagination. They reflect our fears. They expose our inner aspirations. We all feel part of a great drama. At times, we all believe in destiny, consider fate, or consult the stars. We then laugh and say it is nonsense; but we wonder.

When I get angry at something, it is because it has caught me, touched me, troubled me in some way. I cry in a movie because the drama is within me. I am enthused at the victory of another human being because of the personal victories I have known and faced.

In a wonderful TV drama, *Playing for Time*, an argument develops between the Jewish and Polish women who make up the orchestra for the Nazi concentration camp. One Polish prisoner, describing the camp guards, screams, "They are animals!"

The Jewish heroine replies, "That is just the point. They are not animals. If they were animals, we should expect what is happening. The tragedy is that they are human beings, men and women like you and me. It is human beings who are doing these things to us!"

When I am experiencing this kind of drama, I get in touch with the noble side of me that cries against injustice, weeps at the waste, feels sick in the shame. Yet this same experience reveals the brutal Nazi in me, that side of Leo who likes the boots and uniform, who sees the pain and enjoys it, who sees the power and wants it. That is the truth. I have always tried to hide that side of me; now I own it. If I watch a rape scene, I am horrified, disgusted at the violence, and revolted at the forced intimacy. Yet at the same time, the experience reveals a side of me that seeks the fantasy, enjoys the fighting, and revels in the sexual violence. That is the truth.

I have two sides of me. Two heads. Maybe all human beings have two heads. A sick head and a healthy head. One side of us wants to achieve, to be somebody, and to make it in life; however, the other head tells us we are no good, stupid, and unworthy. Many of us cannot accept a compliment because of what the sick head is saying: "You don't deserve it." It is the drama of the sick and healthy going on within, the conflict of light and darkness. It is being an angel in the dirt. The Jekyll-and-Hyde syndrome. Inside is the monster, destructive, diseased, and cruel. Most times, he is kept under control, but at times he breaks out. He looks like me, talks like me, and walks like me. He is a part of me. That dark side of me, that hidden me, and that imperfect me. He is the part of me that needs healing; he is the attitude that needs changing, the ego in me that needs humility.

In the classic *Dr. Jekyll and Mr. Hyde*, we see that Dr. Jekyll appears to control the appearances of Mr. Hyde. Mr. Hyde comes out only when Dr. Jekyll takes the drug. For years, Dr. Jekyll lives his life as a sensitive and caring doctor. Then he decides to reveal his darker side, the evil within. He takes a drug that manifests Mr. Hyde. For a time, Dr. Jekyll seems in control, then one day, one horrid day, the day with which all addicts can identify, the line is crossed. A strange and destructive moment is realized: Mr. Hyde appears in Dr. Jekyll's life without being invited. The power struggle begins. To the complete astonishment of Dr. Jekyll, Mr. Hyde had been quietly and unobtrusively developing strength. Mr. Hyde is the progressive disease. He is now ready for the takeover. Mr. Hyde is in control.

This story is a vivid illustration of the two heads. Mr. Hyde represents the disease. He progressed in strength without the drug, twisting the emotions and feelings of Dr. Jekyll. The line is crossed between abuse and addiction.

TWO HEADS

The tail is now wagging the dog; indeed, the tail is the dog!

Every alcoholic knows this moment. Every drug addict lives this experience. Every gambler remembers. Something is wrong. Things are not going as expected. This moment could take a period of months or years to come into effect, but the shift of power is real.

The choices we make in our lives awaken the disease; the disease feeds on the crazy decisions and insane behavior patterns we live out.

The two heads come into conflict. The diseased head is growing in strength. Sick actions only make him stronger. How do we take away Mr. Hyde's power? First, we must grasp what is happening. Then we add other actions: altering attitudes, changing behaviors, seeking professional help, involving ourselves in Alcoholics Anonymous or a similar program, domestically moving away from our temptations, considering the hidden dangers in our employment, evaluating the kind of friendships we have, connecting with others in recovery, and living one day at a time.

We remove the disease's power by accepting that there

is no cure, but only daily growth that brings its own rewards. We acknowledge aloud that we want recovery more than anything else. We recognize that the disease of obsession and compulsion is the prime problem. We admit that we have become that problem. It is within us. My disease is Leo. I am an alcoholic.

And this daily battle is real. On the way to the therapist, your sick head says: "You don't need therapy. You can control it on your own. Other people have problems without rushing to see a shrink. If you were getting better, you wouldn't need him."

The healthy head tells you not to listen. It remembers the pain that existed before therapy. It tells you to trust the process. The healthy head reminds you of the many joys realized in daily recovery.

It is not only alcoholics or those in therapy who have two heads. In any argument in any home, the heads are battling. *I will not say I'm sorry until he says he's sorry. So they think I'm a child. I'll show them what being irresponsible is. They'll be sorry. I don't know why I married a fool like you. Everybody said you were no good. I wish you were dead.*

Then, after we have banged the door and calmed

down, we ask ourselves, "Did I say all that? Whatever made me say those cruel things?"

Sometimes, the sick head leads to action. The wife is crying and the husband is bleeding. The child trembles with fear as the door opens. The paramedics take the body away. Darkness. Evil. And it emanates from within.

Therapy comes in knowing that the battle is going on. Everybody has crazy moments. Everybody feels like running away or hitting the boss. All children say insensitive things to their parents. Parents say insensitive things to their children. It is part of being imperfect. It is part of being human and not being God; however, when the destructive voices lead to destructive behavior, help is required.

This is why I shared my moment, my car accident, with you. For years, I had listened to my alcoholic head say to the world, "Screw you. I want to drink." For years, I listened to my *ic*. The disease promised he would take away my difference, remove my loneliness and fear, and take away my shame. And for years I believed that crazy and insane *ic*. Then I crashed the car and saw me. I had a moment of sanity. I accepted my alcoholism.

I received treatment in a hospital. They explained the background of my two heads, and they told me I was not alone. *I was not alone.* This I needed to hear. In the hospital therapy groups, I discovered that all the patients had similar messages, and I knew I belonged. From the aged school teacher to the single Polish girl, the pain and sufferings were the same only the locations were different. Know your *ic*. In the hospital, I started to face my disease and began growing up. Spirituality involves knowing that all human beings get crazy now and then. The miracle happened when I could talk about my crazy, sick head. The miracle grew when other people shared their sick heads. We become human when we share our humanness. Share our two heads. This brings a new life that is based upon reality, and it is different from the life many have lived or are living today.

With widespread dishonesty and people pleasing, nobody knows what reality is anymore. People miss what it is to be really human. We cannot love our neighbors because we do not know them. Few know their families and friends. Few people have honest conversations. Few share their fears. Even fewer know themselves. We get exhausted hiding, hence the doctor bills, sedatives, prescription drugs, alcohol cravings, eating binges, even suicide attempts. This constant game playing creates a negative force; it takes us into the darkness.

But here is the good news: we do not have to remain sick. We do not have to remain dishonest. We can choose the creative force, the healthy head. We are creative creatures not conditioned robots. Herein is the miracle of spirituality. To know the Nazi in me is not to *be* the Nazi. To know the aggressor in me is not to *be* the aggressor. To know the sick head is not to *live* in the sick head.

When I was a child, I asked my mother, "How do I become a prince?"

"By thinking noble thoughts," she said.

I still believe that. You become a prince when you think noble and lofty thoughts. Martin Luther King Jr. and Albert Schweitzer were princes, not because they lived in castles or dressed in fine linen, but because they experienced and demonstrated noble thoughts. They lived their dream. They dared others to dream. They lived with and eventually overcame their two heads. They accepted the gift of spirituality from God and dared to risk. They died saying yes to life.

At the end of the day, we do what we want to do. We make our world. We bring into our world what we choose. If we choose a noble life, we will seek noble deeds. If we choose a dishonest life, we will seek dishonest behaviors.

Knowing the existence of my two heads enables me to express the spiritual life.

Surrender to Live

IN THE ANCIENT GREEK theater, actors wore masks to portray different characters and emotions. If you were the villain, you would wear an evil-looking mask; the hero, a handsome mask; and so on. They had masks for every emotion: anger, fear, terror, joy, and happiness.

The performers used the masks to act out a part, to be somebody else, to reveal a feeling. In any one play, an actor could wear many masks. Today, in modern theater, we paint on a face, use special effects to create an illusion, and utilize lighting and music to produce an emotion. Such is drama.

In real life the element of fantasy can be dangerous. We can so easily avoid the symptoms of our diseases or discomforts by seeking escape into fantasy. And in this manipulated dishonesty, the disease grows in strength. We choose to avoid what is happening within us; we prefer illusion, we live in the show, we make a choice for addiction. We may go to work, marry, pay mortgages, have children, receive promotions, sing in church, while always appearing to be fine; but inside, we are dying. We have not faced reality. We have chosen fantasy. We have not surrendered.

Surrender. An interesting word. How many people would connect the word *surrender* with spirituality? However, without surrender, there can be no perceived spirituality. Interestingly enough, the word *Islam* means "to surrender." The word *Muslim* means "one who has surrendered." The prophet Mohammed was concerned about the behavior of his followers when they drank alcohol, so he told them to stop drinking for a period of time before and after fixed religious prayers. The fixed prayer was several times a day. This did not stop the drunkenness. During the free times, many of the Arabs got drunk, becoming cruel and hostile. It was at this point that the prophet forbade the use of alcohol. No Muslim should drink alcohol. They should surrender to a higher authority: the rule of God. Hence, the abstinence is practiced in many Muslim countries.

Occasionally, Christian sects and other religious groups have abstained from alcohol to attain a more productive and spiritual lifestyle; however, abstinence from alcohol is not a part of the Christian tradition.

Surrender happens the moment you open your eyes to see the real you and experience the dynamics of a sickness in your life. Are you drinking too much? Is your marriage working? Is your gambling causing financial problems? How many cigarettes are you smoking, and can you breathe in the morning? Do you eat too much? Is your religion a mask covering a secret life? Are you sick and in need of help? Surrender to the reality of your life. Put aside the fancy talk and lies. Be real.

Here's a tongue-in-cheek story: I am a young soldier in Colonel John Wayne's cavalry troop. We have gone some miles from Fort Apache, and suddenly we are attacked by thousands of screaming Indians. We form a circle at the colonel's command and begin to defend ourselves. More Indians are coming over the hills.

I am afraid. We are powerless over our predicament and our concentration has become unmanageable. I look at the colonel. He looks fierce and is fighting. Still, the Indians attack. More troops are being killed. I am still afraid. I look at the colonel again. He still looks fierce and is fighting. I whisper, "Do you think we should surrender?" I knew I should have waited for a more appropriate time to speak to the colonel!

"So long as the flag is flying, we will be fighting!" he shouts.

At that moment, Sergeant Muggins, whose job is to hold high the flag, falls to the ground, several arrows in his chest. He looks dead.

More Indians pour over the hills. Our situation is becoming more serious by the minute. Only the colonel, a young soldier called Charles, and I are left. Finally, Charles gets an arrow in his rear end!

I look at the colonel. He looks at me.

"Shall we consider surrender?" I say at a quiet moment.

"Americans do not surrender!" he exclaims.

I quickly say, "I'm English. We always surrender."

This seems to reassure him. He reluctantly agrees to surrender. I raise a white handkerchief that I keep for such occasions, and we surrender.

SURRENDER TO LIVE

The message from this crazy story is that people surrender to live!

The word *surrender*, which in my drinking days I

connected with weak people, is the bridge to a deeper understanding of healthy living. It is essential for spiritual growth. When I accept my alcoholism, I surrender to reality, to the painful but life-giving fact that my drinking is never going to be social, and that I will never have complete control over it. So I return to my central point: people surrender to live. In the history of humankind, surrender is usually associated with a desire to stop fighting and to live. In a very real way, surrender is not cowardice, but common sense. It is facing the facts, taking all the aspects of the situation into consideration, and making a decision—a decision to survive. Using the word *surrender* infers that there has been some fight, some conflict, some pain . . . and recovery begins when we realize we cannot survive this way. By stopping the battle, we achieve victory. Hence, we surrender to live.

Most alcoholics have been valiant fighters with their disease for years. They tried to cut down their drinking, change their brand of drinks, limit their drinking to the weekends—in short, they tried everything to be like a social drinker, but because they have a disease, they could never succeed. They are not to blame for being alcoholics. They did not intend to have these problems. They were never ambitious to become alcoholics.

By disease, I mean a deep rooted unease, discomfort, or disconnectedness. A feeling of being not centered, falling apart, a sickness that affects every fiber of our being. In the same way that epilepsy, diabetes, and hypoglycemia are diseases, so is alcoholism. If anything, the emphasis should be on alcoholics taking responsibility for their disease rather than feeling responsible for having it. Ignorant people, religious and medical, who persist in fostering guilt only add insult to injury; they ignorantly hinder the recovery for the alcoholic.

Ignorance has always been the obstacle to healing. For this reason, I maintain that an alcoholic who surrenders to the facts of their disease is neither a coward nor weak, but courageous and realistic. To see things as they are, rather than how we would like them to be, is the discovery of spirituality.

It is suicide to continue fighting when you have no chance of victory. When the writing is on the wall, we do well to heed it. Surrender to the reality and live.

This book is filled with moments when we, nobody

else, must make a decision. The choice is often life or death, destruction or creativity, health or disease, recovery or continued misery. A tragedy is promised in a foolish choice: the decision to have that first drink, a bottle of booze left in the fridge, an evening spent in the company of drinkers instead of going to an AA meeting. The journey toward pain and death start in the foolish choice. The whispered "yes" that should have been "no". We all must face such moments of decision. I stopped fighting alcohol because I could not win. God knows I tried. The arguments, the police arrests, the geographical moves, and the humiliations are there to see. The pain, the loneliness, the fear, and the anger can still be felt. Alcohol always brought me problems. I never went into battle with booze and won. Leo plus alcohol *equals* trouble.

The above fictional story of Colonel Wayne and me explains our resistance to the idea of surrender. We want to be seen as powerful, in control, and in charge with everything working for us. Nothing must be seen as weak, vulnerable, or chaotic—macho men trying to be number one.

According to the book of Genesis, the sin of Adam was wanting to be as God. The Devil tempted Adam and

Eve with the fruit of the tree that would enable them to be like God. Pride, the oldest sin, the fertile foundation for any addiction, to be like God.

> Now the snake was the most cunning animal that the Lord God had made. The snake asked the woman, "Did God really tell you not to eat fruit from any tree in the garden?"
>
> "We may eat the fruit of any tree in the garden," the woman answered, "Except the tree in the middle of it. God told us not to eat the fruit of that tree or even touch it; if we do, we will die."
>
> The snake replied, "That's not true; you will not die." (Gen. 3:1-4)

In Colonel Wayne, we see a man unwilling to face the facts. Miles away from anywhere, the colonel is still trying to impress the general, or his father, or somebody. His pride takes him to the edge of the abyss. His suicidal attempt can be seen in his stubborn battle against overwhelming odds.

In countless wars over many generations, thousands of men and women have died because a few men chose to impress their generals or their fathers. Ego is the real enemy. I have a fantasy that while the colonel and I are knee-deep in Indians, the general back at Fort Apache is eating chicken and planning a vacation. The general is taking care of himself. That is sanity.

I remember during my drinking days wanting to drink like a man, I had long since given up the idea of drinking like a gentleman; however, I always ended up drinking like a drunk. For years, mixing ego with alcohol, I continued to try to drink like a man. Crazy. I talked myself into thinking that people wanted me to drink like a man. Crazy.

I suppose the people I was trying to impress were like the general; they were busy eating chicken and planning vacations, busy taking care of themselves. Sanity. When I stopped drinking for a time, I hated myself. I was ashamed of my inability to drink like other people. I was angry, resentful, bitter, and full of self-pity. This was my brief period of *dryness.* Dryness is not sobriety. Although I was not drinking, I had not accepted my alcoholism. Then the moment of acceptance came after a car crash. I not only accepted my alcoholism, I accepted Leo. I faced the reality of my life.

I am not a musician, painter, skater, chess player, mountaineer, sailor, or mechanic. The list could go on. There are things I can do and things I cannot do. That is life. That is my life. Is it such a big deal that I cannot drink alcohol successfully? Is it? I can live without alcohol.

Of course, every now and again I can return to my pity pot. "Life is unfair." "Misery, I know thee well." "Why did God make me an alcoholic?"

Early in my recovery, I remember thinking that if I became a Roman Catholic priest, the curse of alcoholism might be removed from my life. Then I thought about the Roman Catholic priests I knew and the idea immediately vanished. I never did get around to thinking about being a rabbi!

From this self-indulgent prison, I slowly began to see the real world. I saw children accepting their blindness, disabled children struggling to play in sports, and the blind learning the piano. I saw my mother taking her pill for angina and my father enjoying growing old. I was so preoccupied with what I thought was being taken away from me that I did not recognize what I had been given.

I was drowning in self-pity because I would not let go of the rock of resentment. It was only when I was prepared to let go of the unreal perception of me and my disease that I could heal and begin to live.

When I decided to let go, I developed gratitude . . . a gratitude that grew with my acceptance of myself. People sometimes ask, "What do you mean by *let go*?" I mean talk about the stuff that is unreal, put out that which is untrue, own and discuss the deceit and manipulation, and throw off the masks that keep us hidden. You *let go* to be free. You *let go* to live. You *let go* to be real.

Gratitude flows from that which is given rather from that which is taken. What was taken, we give back. The real we keep.

7

Being Different

'Tis true, my form is something odd,
But blaming me is blaming God;
Could I create myself anew,
I would not fail in pleasing you.

If I could reach from pole to pole,
Or grasp the ocean with a span,
I would be measured by the soul;
The mind's the standard of a man.

Joseph Merrick, "The Elephant Man" [7]

Do you catch the difference in you? Occasionally, as I am going along the road, for no apparent reason I find myself feeling different from other people. I may be at a party and I begin to feel different, or in a church, around a pool, or alone, and I suddenly feel overwhelmingly different.

It is difficult to describe. This feeling is hard to explain, but it is there, always there, though I am not always aware of it. Do you feel different at times?

When I express these feelings to my friends who are recovering alcoholics, they usually say it is because I am alcoholic, that I am getting in touch with my compulsive personality, and that my ego is making me feel different. Yet when I talk with nonalcoholics, they often confide their feelings of difference also.

Does this mean that all alcoholics are the same and yet different from nonalcoholics? Does this mean that the alcoholic is different from other drug addicts, and both are different from nonalcoholics? Are alcoholics the only people with egos? What does it mean to be different?

I do not think I feel different because I am alcoholic.

I suspect that we all feel different at times. We all feel *less than* or *more than* at times.

Let me describe a situation where I feel different, awkward, and uncomfortable, a happening where my difference would make itself felt. Remember, my situation for feeling different will be different from yours, but owning the difference, working through the difference, and accepting the difference can be beneficial. My difference is revealed around alcohol. The difference is not alcohol; the difference is within me. I make the difference. I encounter my individuality in my difference. I encounter my uniqueness in my difference.

Now it is important for you to locate and become aware of when you experience your difference. And what produces the difference for you will be different from others, but the feeling will be the same. It could be food, the color of your skin, sex, not being able to read or write, or alcohol. What brings out your difference?

A situation where I feel different and awkward is at a party where large amounts of alcohol are being served. I look at the other guests and I feel different from them. I know the reason. I accept the reason. My feeling different has to do with my disease. I do not act awkward, but I feel awkward. I want to jump onto the table and ask the guests not to drink too much; however, I'm a liberal. I believe in freedom. They have a right to a hangover!

I begin to notice the signs of feeling awkward. I laugh before the joke is over. I'm dropping peanuts on the floor. Inside me, the fear begins to rise. Yesterday's memories crowd into my mind. I begin to notice how one drunken man holds his glass and how freely he touches and embraces others. My fixed hand around my chin reveals my tension. Most recovering alcoholics feel tense and anxious around people drinking large amounts of alcohol. My feelings are not uncommon.

My difference is alive and kicking.

The other guests see only a good party. I experience fear and looming disaster. In my mind, I project a fight, a neighbor complaining, and police involvement. These feelings do not arise at every party, only where alcohol is being abused.

The drunk has moved to the piano. He has put down his glass. He is balancing a piece of cheese and a small sausage on a paper plate. Another guy is mixing an odd cocktail. I detect a familiar smell coming from the bathroom. Feelings return. Even the sight of a bartender cleaning a glass in a familiar way brings back memories of my difference, memories that are connected with pain, memories that help keep me sober.

In this sense, I am different, not different because I have memories and feelings, but different in the kind of memories and feelings I have. These feelings are the reality and acceptance of my disease, my compulsive and obsessive disease, my alcoholism. But my disease extends beyond an obsession with alcohol. Indeed, I catch my compulsive behavior being activated in other situations—gambling in Las Vegas comes to mind. When I win, I want more. When I lose, I spend more. Always the thrill of possibly winning guides me through the losses. I want it all. Now. In my room afterward, a tired mind replays my mistaken move: "If only I'd taken another card . . ."

Occasionally, my compulsive behavior extends to food and people. I want more food. More people. I become thirsty for friends; I become gluttonous in relationships. All the fears, resentments, and manipulations are involved. I want to fix people, seek to control my calories, eat in my anger, eat after anger. It is the same behavior I exhibited around alcohol. The acting, people pleasing, and hiding all rise up again.

I get in touch with my difference on such situations. These situations are not good or bad, better or worse; they simply reveal my difference. My difference is not the situations, not alcohol, food, gambling, or relationships. The difference is within me.

Why? Because they are real. They are real feelings. They are what is happening in my life. To heal, to recover, I need to know what is happening within me. Owning the feeling is the beginning of action. I make a spiritual move when I accept what is real. The action, the footwork, the healing touch can begin when I accept my difference. I encounter my individuality in my difference. I encounter my uniqueness in my difference.

I DO NOT NEED ALCOHOL TO LIVE

People do not always want you to be different. Other people want us to be the same. No surprises. The ruling majority want people to accept what they accept, believe what they believe, think what they think, and behave like they behave. Most societies are like this. In this way, they structure, organize, and keep control. Difference can be perceived as a threat.

Religion that seeks to establish a code of morality often fears difference. Religion resists miracles that do not fit within an orthodox viewpoint. Religion is suspicious or critical of an artist or thinker who challenges accepted traditions. Why? To avoid involving the church with the religious crank, the pious fake, or the popular charlatan. In this way, religion and the church seek to remain honorable and pure. Remember, not many yesterdays ago, unscrupulous people, desirous of power, would manipulate tricks to indicate divine intervention and miracle. For this reason, even the saintly mystics were investigated.

This was the tragedy of Joan of Arc. Her rigorous honesty and truthfulness would not allow her to be helped into religious approval, even when the religious approval would give her freedom. When she was being investigated by the bishop who was trying to spare her from being burned at the stake for saying that she had heard God's voice, he asked, "Don't you think it could be your imagination?"

Joan thought for a moment and then replied, "Yes, it was my imagination."

The bishop breathed a sigh of relief. He thought to himself, *Thank God, we can save her from the fires.*

However, Joan of Arc continued, "It was my imagination because that is the way that God speaks to me."

Joan's difference can be seen in her imagination, in her awareness of God's voice, and in her believing that she was chosen by God. To the religious authorities, she was crazy, arrogant, and demonic.

That is why I argue for a free and diversified appreciation of spirituality, which need not conform with any one religion or religious viewpoint. As we see in Joan of Arc's experience, spirituality can be revealed in our imaginations. Indeed, the church can be wrong. Religious attitudes can be wrong. The powerful majority can be wrong. Some might argue that in the story of Joan, we are seeing again the trial of Jesus. The condemnation of the different? The crucifixion of God's miracle?

Let's go back to that party I described earlier in this

chapter. One drunk is vomiting and the other is still mixing odd cocktails. Now that I own my awkwardness and discomfort, I can leave and go home. I wasn't enjoying the party anyway. Alternatively, my difference could easily be unhealthily attracted to what is happening. I could *drink in* the situation and enjoy the drinking and chaotic behavior. I could even start to enjoy my resentments and superior attitude. Creating a judge and victim situation for myself, I would be choosing to stay in the sickness to condemn the sickness!

I could want a drink—not have a drink, but want a drink. I could want the fantasy back, seek the attention, and experience through others the alcoholic escape.

In every home, office, or school, the temptation to do what others want is served up in a variety of ways, all carrying their own subtle guilt trip if refused. The message is always the same: Be what others want. Say what the crowd wants to hear. Exchange your hard-won dignity for the quick applause.

We are told that to be different is to separate from the herd. Most believe what they are told. It is easier to join the crowd than fight the criticism. People often exchange their difference for any easy life.

But is it easy? What about the fight going on within?

In some respects, we are all different. Somewhere in all of us is an addiction, compulsion, or obsession screaming to be heard. At times, we hide our difference. Some people die never revealing their difference. They die not being known. How can this be easy?

Once you begin to face your difference and accept it within yourself, it becomes harder and more painful to live the lie of denial. The price of pleasing people gets to be too much. Think how much effort, energy, and personal suffering goes into seeking to please everyone. It is okay for me to say *no*. I do not need permission from others to live.

I knew about a lady who was knocked off of her bicycle by a car. It was the driver's fault for not stopping, yet she apologized and tried to cycle home.

A man confided in me that he felt guilty making an emergency call to the fire department when his garage caught fire. He didn't like disturbing them on a Saturday night!

Think of the suicides. Imagine the guilt feelings expressed in the farewell notes: "I do not wish to be a burden any longer, and so . . ." "Nobody understands how lonely and different I feel; therefore, I have . . ." "I cannot please everyone and so I've decided to end my life . . ."

It is refreshing to meet an individualist, a person willing to say *no* or "I don't want to do that."

Part of the attraction of the man Gandhi was that he believed in and respected his individuality. He could live with difference. He owned his difference. He would not accept or condone intolerance and bigotry. He represented to the world God's gift of freedom to humankind. Any form of slavery was abhorrent to him. He believed that nobody can imprison, beat, or kill the human spirit. His spirituality and tolerance are captured in his statement "An eye for an eye makes the whole world blind." Our human soul lives within our difference, our uniqueness, and our specialness. Our spirituality is in our difference. You cannot arrest, chain, hurt, or kill my difference, because it does not belong to you. It comes from God. In God, I am different and unique. We need to accept this gift.

Let us take an aspect of difference that many deny and run away from: gayness. In no way do I consider gayness a disease or a sickness. I am using it simply as an example of difference. Thousands of people are in denial of their gayness. They refuse to face, accept, and own their true selves, their true sexuality, and their true feelings. Many grow up feeling different and live the lie of hiding their difference. It leads to a tragic pain.

The suppression and fear of homosexuality can lead to the disease of homophobia, which is destructive and will eventually suffocate our God-given spirituality. It is a kind of sexual anti-Semitism. Homophobia is like any other form of obsession and compulsion in that it feeds on denial, anger, loneliness, and manipulation. It afflicts those who beat up gays. It afflicts those who are forever criticizing and speaking against gays. It afflicts those wanting to know who is gay in the workplace. These people, if asked, would maintain that they are revealing a normal interest in a serious problem! Hate and prejudice feed the disease of homophobia. The long-term goals are divisive and destructive. Homophobia often masks homosexual feelings, reflecting personal pain and self-hatred. As with the disease of addiction, the dynamics need to be understood. The homophobic needs to be loved and understood, and gently led to self-acceptance and integration.

Those writers involved in the study of human sexuality often prefer the word *gayness* to homosexuality because it means more than sexual activity. Gayness is saying more about a person than what happens in bed. Gayness involves bringing homosexual feelings into a concern for politics, the world, art, and literature. Gayness has that spiritual dimension that adds soul to life.

In *The Angel and the Frog*, a fable about animals who reveal the dysfunction that exists in our society and our personal lives, I write about Old John, the mule who describes his personal healing from homophobia in connection with two Burmese gay cats, Chico and Chandu.

"I used to think that I didn't understand your kind of love. But that is not true. Love is love. None of us loves the same way. We are different, even those of us who belong to the same breed. Our love is different but it is the same."

Continuing to speak directly to Chandu and Chico, Old John continued, "I was jealous of your love. I admired the way you could kiss, hug, and laugh in front of the other animals. I imagined that it was Elizabeth and me. But then I'd come back to earth and I was alone.

"I watched you both when Alice was speaking. Please,

try not to be upset by what you heard. You are not the cause of this trouble. You both loved Snake. Snake loved you. Your love helped him feel better." Old John paused, searching for the right words.

"Take it from me, it doesn't matter how much you love if you can't say it. *You gotta show love*. You gotta tell them. That's what you guys do. You're not afraid to show your love. And I think that makes everyone different when they're around you. Snake was different when he was with you. I know I feel different when I'm with you." Old John smiled fondly at the cats who sat hugging each other, smiling through their tears.

Old John took another deep breath. He rarely spoke more than a few sentences at a time, and he had never spoken with such heartfelt emotion. "I was afraid to show my love, and so I felt stupid when I was with Elizabeth. I felt stupid for not knowing the fancy love-words and I'd get angry at Elizabeth. But when I'm with you two, I'm not afraid. You're showing me how to love. I think that scares many of us. We don't know how to show love, so we get insecure and make showing love somehow wrong." Cedric, Timothy, and Muriel nodded in agreement.

"Don't let them chase you away. We need you. We need you to show us how to love." In his deep, soulful voice, Old John then started to sing what he had sung during the Gratitude Service, only now it took on deeper meaning.

Hear the silence growing, in each and every heart.
See the love-glow growing, never to depart.
We are ONE together, knowing we are free.
Let it be. Let it be.

If you are homophobic and in denial, then, as I've said concerning the alcoholic, you need to accept it. Gay feelings do not go away. Being gay is who you are. You can pretend to date girls and please your family; you could get married and have children; you could spend your life being what you are not. But it is still a lie.

So what if you are different? Your sexuality is a statement of who you are. The variety of God's creation will always baffle and confuse.

Your sexuality can be creative and loving or corrupt and diseased. Gay or heterosexual, the temptations are the same. Reality or fantasy, which will it be? The wrong choice is a decision for the disease, for the compulsion, and for the obsession. Alongside this choice: anger, resentment, isolation, fear, or cruel indifference. There is another way: expressed feelings that reveal vulnerability of love, revealed courage and risk, and shared truthfulness that enables privileged listeners to locate their own forgotten difference.

In the difference is the many. In the many is the ONE. Gay relationships, like heterosexual relationships, will grow in an atmosphere of honest and creative acceptance. What started as difference becomes God's creative diversity. That is spirituality.

I am not afraid of my difference anymore. It is not a barrier, but a bridge to divine understanding. My being an alcoholic, having a disease, and being a minority connects me with others who are different. I'm able to understand others who have been misunderstood.

I am discovering that only my outsides look different from yours. My insides, my God-given spirituality, is the same. When I read about the death of John Merrick, the Elephant Man, I feel his difference. I can identify.

Some six months after Merrick's return from the country, he was found dead in bed. This was April 1890. He was lying on his back as if asleep, and had evidently died suddenly and without a struggle, since not even the cover-let of the bed was disturbed. The method of his death was peculiar. So large and so heavy was his head that he could not sleep lying down. When he assumed the recumbent position, the massive skull was inclined to drop backwards, with the result that he experienced no little distress. The attitude he was compelled to assume when he slept was very strange. He sat up in bed with his back supported by pillows, his knees were drawn up, and his arms clasped round his legs, while his head rested on the points of his bent knees.

He often said to me that he wished he could lie down to sleep "like other people." I think on his last night, he must, with some determination, have made the experiment. The pillow was soft, and the head when placed on it, must have fallen backwards and caused a dislocation of the neck. Thus it came about that his death was due to the desire that had dominated his life—the pathetic, but hopeless desire to be "like other people."[8]

Perhaps in the end, John Merrick could not accept his difference. He died trying to be the same. Although he had been courageous with his disease, noble in his attitudes, loving and vulnerable in his lifestyle, still that small part of his obsession and compulsion got him in the end. That part of him that was his difference, inability to sleep like others, he would not own. It made him attempt the unreal. It made him live for a moment the fantasy. John died trying to be like you and me. His final act of desperate people-pleasing killed him.

As Shakespeare wrote, "We know what we are, but not what we may be."

Meditation

THE KEY TO SERENE living is an awareness of yourself. The miracle is within. Meditation is an aid that many use to achieving serenity and peace of mind.

Addiction is escape. It is choosing fantasy instead of reality, wanting to be somebody else, pretending to be happy when you are sad, and appearing in control when you are falling apart inside. Some drink to avoid problems; perhaps a student uses marijuana to please his friends; a person eats often behind anger or boredom. Drugs supposedly take the pain out of life, but in reality they progressively create havoc. Addiction involves loneliness, isolation, and a constant feeling of feeling less than.

Unfortunately, meditation is seen by some to be an escape from life, a trip into nirvana, or a journey from the material world into a transcendental bliss, a kind of spiritual high. Christian mystics and Eastern gurus have occasionally presented the view that our bodies, the world, and this life are sick and corrupt.

BE STILL AND KNOW THAT I AM GOD

We can escape from the restrictions of the physical body by the use of meditation. Many people over the years have disappeared into the deserts and mountains or entered temples and ashrams to find a peace that they believed could not be experienced in ordinary living. They closed the door on their old lives, they left behind family and friends, and they sought meaning elsewhere. Not everybody, thank God, sees meditation in this exclusive way, but still many fear and avoid meditation because of where it might lead. An English friend once said to me, "Meditation is decidedly foreign. Not to be done in polite society. Rather like sex, it scares the horses!"

In my opinion, the truth is the opposite: it does not scare the horses, and we should not be afraid of it. Meditation is a technique for realizing our full potential as human beings and living our lives to the fullest. It is about finding the time and discovering the energy to be. It is placing the physical, mental, and emotional aspects of our lives in an *at-one-ment*. It is using silence to say yes. Meditation is a part of the God-given gift of spirituality. It is feeling who we are and expressing it in the world. It is exploring the reality of the present. Meditation has much to say to the alcoholic, drug addict, and overeater, but it is also a technique that would benefit everybody. With meditation comes acceptance, growth, and serenity.

It is not just for religious people or priests, rabbis, mullahs, monks, nuns, gurus, and eccentrics in the desert. Meditation is for shy Alice in the grocery shop; Johnny, who is angry at the world because his parents are divorced; Ann, who is recovering from anorexia; Jack, who is facing cancer; and young Harry, a drug addict who is contemplating suicide. Meditation is for Bill and Carol, who are very busy people and are planning a family; George and Phillip, who celebrate a ten-year relationship together; Henry, a widower who feels alone. Meditation fits life.

We should not think that meditations are for the favored few. We exclude joy from our world because we think and feel most things are not for us. We also foolishly segregate life into compartments, pigeonholes, or boxes and we remain impoverished. We decided meditation is for saints, clever people, religious, fanatics, or eccentrics. *Yes, it is for these . . . and you.* We think that to meditate, you must wear funny clothes, say Hindu words, kneel for hours, burn incense in your room, fast on bread and

water, avoid sex, or use mantras. It can involve these . . .
but more. Truth is always in the more. You do not need
to study spiritual books, pass religious examinations, or
have a pronounced longing for God to meditate. You
need only a desire. Meditation allows for the experience
of God and life. It allows you to experience you.

What is meditation? *Webster's Dictionary* defines meditation as "a deep reflection on sacred matters as a devo-
tional act"; however, meditation is not so much about
doing, getting, or achieving something as it is about
being, experiencing, and discovering ourselves.

Meditation relives the tremendous truth depicted by
Michaelangelo on the Sistine Chapel ceiling in Rome,
where God is touching or has touched the fingertip of
Adam. At that point, the spark of the divine is given. In
the created is the Creator, the miracle of being human.
In the discovery of ourselves, we will ultimately find God.
"Be still, and know that I am God" (Ps. 46:10 KJV).

As the psalmist wrote,

"Be still, and know that I am God."

"Be still, and know . . ."

"Be still . . ."

"Be . . ."

Meditation is a technique. Certain actions or procedures should be taken to aid relaxation, awareness, and stillness. The obvious needs to be said: proper rest and diet are necessary. Balance, rest, and nutrition are important prerequisites for any meditation exercise. This is essential for the recovering addict.

How long should you meditate? When you are beginning, a few minutes will be enough. Remember, most of us tend to be obsessive and compulsive about achieving something, which will sabotage our meditation techniques. In the first few months, ten minutes or less will be sufficient. After experiencing meditation, the length of time will vary, but the qualitative consistency will remain constant.

A. "Be Still" Technique

Go to a place where you can be alone. Make yourself comfortable.

Be still.

To get to inner peace, we must first listen to the world.

Hear the noises that surround your life: cars, birds, rain, people shouting in the streets. After listening to these noises for a few moments, leave them outside and listen to the noises within your room. Concentrate on the clock ticking, fridge buzzing, fire crackling, dog sighing. Then come from the noises in your room to yourself. Spend a few moments enjoying and exploring yourself. Touch your legs, thighs, stomach, arms, neck and face. You are important. Remind yourself you are unique, special, and divine. The breath of God was first breathed into Adam, and now it breathes in you. Hear yourself breathing. Feel yourself breathing. Relax in your breathing. Be still.

B. Gratitude Technique

Do the "Be Still" technique, then:

Focus on a part of your body or an aspect of creation that you enjoy. Either look at it, touch it, or imagine it. Be grateful.

I've used this technique to be grateful for family, a sunset, rolling hills, the ocean, a friend.

C. Word Technique

Do the "Be Still" technique, then:

Bring into your mind a word you value. For a few moments, quietly say the word, explore the word, bring energy into that word.

I've used: joy, peace, love, family names.

The use of a mantra, a chosen word, or sound that means something to only you can be used with this technique. Although the use of a mantra is Hindu, it has been found to be helpful for people with other religious backgrounds or none. Also, the word *namaste* comes to mind. It is used for many people who have heard it spoken in the Far East. It means "the God in me celebrates the God in you." But it is used by many who do not know what it means, who appreciate the sacred sound. Anything that makes sense to you and is positive can be used.

D. Breathing Technique

Do the "Be Still" technique, then:

Concentrate on breathing in and out. Feel your body

breathing. Experience the breathing. Slowly mouth a word that fits your rhythm. Breathe that word into your being. Let that energy breathe through your body. Example: so-ber, so-ber, so-ber.

My breathing words are: hon-esty, se-ren-ity, Je-sus, ho-ly.

Remember, meditation is an experience; the experience involves you. Meditation is real and it has been given to us over the years. It is an ancient technique for achieving peace and serenity.

With the aid of meditation, I can feel alive without the need to drink alcohol, smoke a joint, or use a drug. And everything I experience is real. Meditation enables me to live with all the various aspects of my life: when I am tense, anxious, lonely, or afraid; when I am creating, writing articles, preparing a sermon, or lecturing patients; and even when I am playing, walking along the beach or enjoying friendships. Meditation awakens that spark of the divine that exists within me and holds it in my life. Meditation reminds me that my space is my home.

Many people know "The Serenity Prayer." I have found it helpful to take a phrase or word from it and use it in any of the above meditation techniques. Here is the complete prayer:

The Serenity Prayer

God grant me the serenity
to accept the things I cannot change;
courage to change the things I can;
and wisdom to know the difference.

Living one day at a time;
Enjoying one moment at a time;
Accepting hardship as the pathway to peace;
Taking, as He did, this sinful world
as it is, not as I would have it;

Trusting that He will make all things right,
if I surrender to His Will;
That I may be reasonably happy in this life
and supremely happy with Him
forever in the next.
Amen.

Reinhold Niebuhr

9

Relationships

THE SPIRITUAL LIFE TEACHES US that we are powerful human beings. We make the difference in the living of our lives. We are capable of creating a healthier life, healthier relationships, and a healthier world.

We are not automated robots but spiritual creatures who have the power to determine our destiny. In the living of our lives, we create success or failure. Nothing just happens. Things happen as a direct result of the decisions, actions, and beliefs we manifest in our lives. This is an important awareness, and it can make all the difference to our recovery and continued recovery.

In Chapter 3 I told the story of the two little fish that were afraid to swim out into the ocean. They huddled together in fear and as a result missed life. We can do this in relationships. The fear of being rejected, the fear of not being good enough, or the fear of not being able to sustain a relationship keeps us victims of loneliness and isolation. Often we seem to prefer the security of loneliness to the risked possibility of happiness. When we first hear this sentence, it sounds crazy. How could anyone prefer painful isolation to the creative possibility of a loving relationship? But fear creates atrophy. We become immobile. We isolate ourselves.

We must place this understanding of fear in the context of an increasingly addictive society. Fear is a symptom of addiction. It is a symptom of codependency. It is a symptom of those millions of children who grew up in dysfunctional homes. In the chaos of addiction, with its associated reverberations throughout family, church, and society, many are affected. Few people are spared. We live in an addicted society.

Just consider some of the addictions and compulsive

behaviors that exist: alcoholism; drug addiction; gambling; men and women who love too much; compulsive overeating with its related disorders of diets, use of diuretics or laxatives, and self-induced vomiting; religious addiction; sexual addiction; compulsive spending; obsessive physical exercise; workaholism; prescription drug abuse; social media obsession; codependency symptoms; and other abuse issues related to all of the above. Then add the millions of children who become dysfunctional as a result of growing up in these addicted and abusive homes. Is anyone spared?

If you have to take a drug, look a certain way, have a relationship to be somebody, then the fear of not being good enough, having enough, or looking good enough will affect the living of your life, and the spiritual power of self-acceptance is lost.

Relationships obviously are affected. The major areas of relationships are: a) ourselves, b) other people, and c) God.

Although I have placed God last in the order of significant relationships, it does not mean that I consider our relationship with God the least important. On the contrary, I consider our relationship with God (as we understand God) to be essential, pervasive, and the key to the discovery of the spiritual life; however, it is also my belief that God is manifested in this world, in creation, in people. If we do not develop a relationship with ourselves, if we do not embark on the journey into self, then I do not believe we can comprehend the reality of God in our lives.

God has chosen to work through people, prophets, seers, writers, priests, musicians, artists, scientists, psychologists, lovers, and friends. Because God is truly involved in creation, the exercise of human relationships and communication, then it follows that God is demonstrated in the living of our lives. In our relationships with other people, we hear the promises of God. Therefore, when we have developed a healthy relationship with ourselves and other people, we are ready to meaningfully apprehend our relationship with God.

Without relationships, we cannot live effectively. We may exist, painfully, but we will never experience the abundance of the spiritual life. Only when we feel good about ourselves, and ourselves in relationship to others, will we be able to understand what it means to be an essential part of God's creation. The energizing joy of self-love creates healthy relationships with others. Therefore, in our pursuit of the spiritual life, we need to consider relationships.

A healthy relationship within ourselves is essential for the living of the spiritual life. We exchange life for existence when we isolate; the impetus for creative living exists within ourselves. As we have said earlier in this book, the miracle is within. We are the miracle. We are the center of our universe. Everything that is created emanates from within. The God of our understanding is dependent on our willingness and determination to discover God in our world. Our relationships with lovers, family, friends, and associates is dependent on the attitudes we adopt. Our influence on the neighborhood, job market, and society is dependent on the apprehension of our spiritual power. Relationships emanate from self!

The spiritual life creates healthy relationships. Loving relationships do not just happen. There is an art to love. As with so many aspects of living, we need to develop an expertise in achieving responsibility, confidence, and consistency. Nobody just starts playing the piano. We must practice, learn the language of music, comprehend what we are doing wrong, and develop skills to improve style and performance. The joy of being a pianist is the result of work and effort.

No one just sits down and starts writing poetry for the first time. Poets need to develop their craft. They need to finely tune their feelings for words, sentence construction, and the form in which they wish to write. Poets must spend time with the tools of their artistry, selecting carefully those words that have an inner resonance to convey their message. Poetry is an art that requires effort.

The art of developing a relationship is the same. Relationships are more than casual acquaintances. They involve the desire to know and be known. They require a willingness to understand and be understood. Relationships take time to develop and a learning process is involved in each relationship. Mistakes will be made. Because human beings are not God, our relationships will not always be perfect. Yet our desire to develop the spiritual life requires that we seek a personal improvement that leads to health and recovery. Remember, we desire to be the best human beings we can be, developing the best loving relationships we can achieve.

How do we develop a guide to healthy, loving, and meaningful relationships? It is a common maxim that we learn from our mistakes. Acknowledged mistakes can become the focal point for improvement. In the dynamic concept of surrender, admitting our faults, and accepting our involvement in dysfunctional behavior, we begin the process of recovery—spiritual recovery. Therefore, when we become honestly aware of the problems in our relationship, we grasp the possibility for healing.

For those who work a twelve-step program, as written in the Alcoholics Anonymous book, this understanding might offer a creative insight into the phrase *turn it over*. The emphasis is on making the decision to run our lives in a new direction. The responsibility for turning it over rests in our decision, willingness, or desire to risk taking a different direction in life. But before we can turn ourselves in a different direction, we need to know which way we are facing. We must understand *west* before we can know *east*. We need to know *in* before we can get *out*. We need to know *sick* before we can get *well*.

Let us look at some of the characteristics that create unhealthy relationships:

Narrow, Bigoted, Controlling

A relationship cannot develop and grow if it excludes the possibility of change. Many relationships die because they create the atmosphere of a prison; life becomes a chained existence rather than an experience of unlimited possibilities. The fear of confronting the new and unfamiliar makes some people seek control. The fear of people, places, and things that are different produces a prejudiced and narrow outlook on life.

Isolate, Selfish, Resentful

It is emotionally painful to live with someone who isolates and who does not want to be known. People can use silence as a weapon to abuse their partners; it becomes a passive form of anger. A cruel selfishness is involved in this silent torture. An unwillingness to share reveals buried resentments but also creates resentments in others.

Aggressive, Angry, Jealous

The root of so much aggression and anger is fear. The fear may be the result of childhood issues or drug-related symptoms; however, the need to dominate the relationship through violence often can be a motivating factor. Here we have an example of fear creating anger or violence that eventually destroys the possibility of a relationship.

Low Self-Esteem, Lies, Manipulation, People-Pleasing

You cannot please all the people all of the time. If one or both partners in a relationship are so lacking in self-worth, then they create only the illusion of success, happiness with lies and manipulation. The relationship becomes another facet of this dysfunctional illusion. Honesty is the basis of any healthy relationship.

Rigid, Uncompromising, Proud, Arrogant

Any relationship requires willingness to bend. We are not God, and to refuse to compromise in life is to destroy any possibility of dialogue. The tragedy is that the proud person is in emotional pain but refuses to express their need of others. Such rigidity bleeds feelings from any relationship.

Egotistical, Thoughtless, Spoiled

Many children who are spoiled by their parents, given everything they ever wanted at their slightest whim, grow up to be selfish. They become lost and hurt in a world that refuses to respond to their wants or needs like their doting parents did. Such people are unable to create a healthy relationship; their obsessive infatuation with their needs eventually destroys them.

Emotionally Cold, Unaffectionate, Detached, Unresponsive

Many adults who were hurt in their childhoods, having been emotionally and sexually abused, often are unable to create intimacy in a relationship. The past abuse haunts them into adulthood, making them prisoners of an unresponsiveness that keeps other people locked out.

Isolated, Uncommunicative, Lonely, Boring

All relationships are based on people wanting to come together, to know and be known. To isolate or restrict communication eventually destroys a relationship. Self-induced isolation also creates a boring loneliness that keeps people away, because there is nothing adventuresome, exciting, or attractive about the life they are living.

Health Problems (Hungry, Angry, Lonely, Tired)

A healthy person has the possibility of being an exciting person. To neglect health through poor diet, repressed feelings, self-induced isolation, and an abuse of work or sleep is an escape from reality; it also is spiritually irresponsible. Our physical, emotional, and mental well-being is our responsibility as creative people; to neglect important health issues is to hinder the possibility of healthy relationships.

Negative, Destructive, Cynical, Pessimistic

Any healthy relationship is a positive statement about life. To develop negative and pessimistic attitudes only destroys the creative momentum for a relationship.

SPIRITUALITY IS BEING FREE

In my daily meditation book, *Say Yes to Your Life*, I wrote this about relationships:

Spirituality is about being willing to reach out into new areas, engage in new and different relationships, and enjoy the richness of God's world.

As I grow in sobriety, I develop the capacity

```
to react differently to painful situations and
overcome them. I learn that mistakes can make
for new conquests. Lasting joys and achieve-
ments are born in the risk.⁹
```

We now have clearly seen the characteristics that create dysfunctional relationships. All of the above characteristics would destroy any relationship with ourselves, other people, and God.

How can we claim to love God if by our attitudes and behavior we are destroying any meaningful relationship with other people? How can we grow and develop spiritually as human beings if we have isolated ourselves from any creative relationship? God is discovered through our relationship with ourselves and others.

In confronting the characteristics of a dysfunctional relationship, we are able to identify the goals for developing and sustaining healthy relationships. We can only turn it over when we see what needs to be changed. In confronting dysfunction, we are brought into the joy of spiritual recovery.

Suggestions for a healthy relationship with ourselves, other people, and God:

1. Accept criticism gratefully; appreciate the opportunity to improve.

2. Do not indulge in self-pity.

3. Do not expect special consideration from anyone.

4. Seek to express your feelings responsibly.

5. Realize that no person or situation is wholly good or bad.

6. Experience defeat and disappointment without whining or complaining.

7. Do not worry unduly about things that are not your responsibility.

8. Do not boast in a socially unacceptable way.

9. Enjoy the success and good fortune of others.

10. Remain open-minded and listen to the opinions of others.

11. Do not harbor resentments.

12. Remember that we are not God.

10

Relapse and Treatment

RELAPSE IS A PROGRESSIVE behavioral pattern that, if not confronted, will lead to dysfunctional living, either a return to alcoholic drinking, use of mind-altering chemicals, destructive eating patterns, sexually acting out, workaholism, compulsive gambling, codependent behavior, or the myriad of painful behaviors and feelings that adult children have sought to recover from. In a sentence, relapse results in addictive or destructive behavior.

Spirituality is the antidote to relapse, because the power of knowing that we are creative children of God, as we understand God, becomes the positive factor that enables recovery. Spirituality is knowing, on a daily basis, that we are positive and creative human beings and that we have the capacity, which has been given by God in creation, to arrest dysfunctional behavior. We are the miracle. We make the difference. In the living of our lives, God is activated.

In their pioneer book on relapse prevention, *Staying Sober,* authors Terence T. Gorski and Merlene Miller write:

Recovery from addiction is like walking up a down escalator. It is impossible to stand still. When you stop moving forward, you find yourself moving backward. You do not have to do anything in particular to develop symptoms that lead to relapse. All you need to do is to fail to take recovery steps. The symptoms develop spontaneously in the absence of a strong recovery program. Once you abandon a recovery program, it is only a matter of time until the symptoms of past acute withdrawal appear, and if nothing is done to manage them, you will experience a period

of out-of-control behavior that we call the
relapse syndrome. Loss of control of past
acute withdrawal symptoms results in the
relapse syndrome.[10]

The book emphasizes that developing a strong and comprehensive recovery program is a plea for spirituality: spirituality is recovery. The awareness that we make the difference in our lives, that things begin to happen when we activate them in our daily decisions, that wellness is directly related to attitudinal and behavioral changes we are prepared to make: this constitutes a spiritual awakening.

What does the concept of relapse mean as it relates to chemical addiction and compulsive behavior? It does not simply mean returning to alcoholic drinking or mind-altering drug use. Just as we have begun to understand that sobriety is more than not drinking, so relapse is a progressive pattern that leads to negative and destructive behaviors, *and the person may not have returned to active drug use*. It is certainly true that many people who are caught in the relapse syndrome do return to chemical usage, but it is important to remember that people can be in a state of relapse for many years and not be using any mind-altering drug. Indeed, they may never use; however, and this cannot be stressed enough, they are not experiencing the joy, freedom, and creativity of sobriety.

The relapse syndrome does not only apply to alcoholism and drug use. The relapse process is applicable to all dysfunctional lifestyles that have previously sought a recovery program. Those at risk will include alcoholics, drug users, bulimics, prescription drug users, sex addicts, workaholics, religious addicts, men and women who love too much, nicotine addicts, compulsive gamblers, codependents to all these compulsive behaviors, plus the millions of adult children who grew up in these dysfunctional homes. It is not too extravagant to suggest that society is often at various stages of relapse. Government agencies, school boards, industry, and the church can share the relapse symptoms of denial that make them minimize the damage that addiction is causing in our society. We are all at risk.

Because relapse is an addictive process, it has symptoms, characteristics, or signs that reveal its presence. Our spiritual recovery rests in recognizing and confronting these symptoms.

Those in relapse will begin to exhibit the behavior patterns and attitudes that they practiced when they were using drugs or were dysfunctional. The relapse person is moving backward toward a powerless and unmanageable life.

These high risk characteristics include:

A. Negative Attitudes and Behaviors

1. Inappropriate expressions of anger, violence, sarcasm, rudeness, selfishness, and thoughtlessness

2. Unwillingness to resolve guilt and shame issues

3. Extreme feelings of helplessness and hopelessness

4. Unrealistic fears and anxieties

5. Extreme nervousness and tension in non-threatening situations

6. Boredom with recovery program and life in general

7. No creative or satisfying leisure interest

8. A denial or minimizing of past problems

9. A recognizable and continuing depression

10. A development of cross-addictive behavior patterns, such as gambling, sex, food, and work

11. Exhibiting long periods of exhaustion, fatigue, and apathy

12. Impatient with recovery program and life; nothing happening quickly enough

13. Progressive isolation from recovery people

14. A preoccupation with past dysfunctional behavior(s)

15. Unwilling to express or deal with resentments

B. Problems in Relationships That Relate to Relapse

1. Argumentative with others

2. Difficulty experienced in meeting new friends and developing relationships

3. Unwillingness to trust others

4. Isolation from recovering friends

5. Friendships developed with people who have dysfunctional behavioral patterns

6. Sexual problems such as fear of sex, impotence, lack of control concerning sexual feelings, inappropriate sexual behavior

7. Inability to handle responsibilities with family or friends

C. High Pressure Situations

1. Difficulty coping with unemployment or success

2. Difficulty handling evenings or weekends

3. Overwhelmed by the ordinary stresses and anxieties of life

4. Lack of objectives or goals in life

5. Inability to cope with physical pain or problems

6. Desire to be surrounded by alcohol or past dysfunctional behavior(s)

Spiritual Recovery Program

The key to recovery from relapse is to recognize these symptoms and confront them, talk about them, and deal with them. Some people might need to return to treatment for their relapse issues. Others should contact a relapse therapist. But for many, it will mean returning to a twelve-step program that previously brought relief from their addictive and compulsive behaviors. Perhaps for those who refused to get involved in a twelve-step program, the time for surrender has arrived. This fellowship is about making decisions that lead to change, and the spiritual awakening comes in knowing we can achieve recovery.

For anyone who recognizes some of the relapse symptoms that have been discussed above, the time to act is now; procrastination is not only dangerous, it is a symptom of relapse. Recovery is a process, not an event. It is a circle, not a straight line. We can return to the beginning of our spiritual recovery.

You might say this is easier said than done. But is it easier to go back to the pain, powerlessness, and unmanageability of past behaviors? I believe it is easier to get healthy than it is to remain dysfunctional. Why? Because compulsive and obsessive behaviors are destructive, destroying every area of life and personal happiness. People relapse because they choose to forget their past pain, minimizing the consequences of their addictions, denying the tragedies of their past.

Elie Weisel, the famous Jewish poet and philosopher, was asked, "Why do you keep talking and writing about the Holocaust?" His reply was pertinent to this discussion: "If people are not reminded, if people choose to forget the tragedy of the Holocaust and its effects on and for humanity, then it will all come back."

This is also true for relapse. The relapse syndrome is a series of progressive choices to escape the reality of our true selves, our true natures, who we really are. Relapse is a cunning and powerful aspect of denial.

Spirituality is about reality. It is about taking responsibility as creative creatures for the quality of our lives, the quality of our relationships, and the quality of our world. Spirituality confronts and stops our dance into death.

Spirituality is our "yes" to life. It is knowing that God loves us enough to be involved in our lives. It is understanding that whatever the problems might be, we have the capacity within ourselves to seek and find the solution. Spirituality is recognizing divinity in the choices we make, the decisions we implement in our lives.

For many years, people have talked about the program of recovery as being spiritual, emphasizing that there is not a spiritual aspect to the program, but the whole program is spiritual. If this is true for recovery, it must also be true in treatment, because it is in treatment that recovery (hopefully) begins.

Earlier in this book, I sought to make the important distinction between spirituality and religion, between denominationalism and the all-inclusive power of spirituality. Many people have been helped to understand the difference by this important but succinct saying: "Religion is man-made; spirituality is God-given."

The essential contribution that spirituality makes in the treatment process concerns God's indiscriminate love; nobody is excluded. God really does love all creation equally, in spite of our imperfections. We no longer need to look at life from the outside; we are created to be involved.

This is a very important message for all addicts, codependents, and adult children to hear: regardless of race, culture, sexual orientation, or dysfunction, we are loved by God. Now we need to begin to love ourselves. This spiritual message needs to be at the core of all aspects of treatment.

It has been my experience that although many treatment centers believe that spirituality is the key ingredient to recovery, still the language used and ideas conveyed are suspiciously religious. Often their themes for meditation and prayer are exclusively biblical:

Moses escaping slavery in Egypt

Cain and Abel—depicting jealousy

David and Goliath—overcoming incredible odds

The Sermon on the Mount

The miracles of healing

The prodigal son

Jesus dying that we might live

The new life of the resurrection

The Lord's Prayer is used as the prayer for recovery, unconsciously disregarding the fact that many people in treatment are Jewish, agnostic, atheist, or from other religions. Words are used in prayer and meditation that are specifically religious and cannot be understood without a knowledge of Judeo-Christian theology. Examples include: grace, soul, redemption, confession, sin, testimony, absolution, Savior, discipleship, and remnant.

I am not suggesting that the above cannot have an important role to play in the discovering and nurturing of the spiritual life, but the words and phrases need explaining; more specifically, they need to be understood within the context of a recovery program. Also, scriptural stories and references need to be supplemented with secular words and stories that are less offensive or scary to many people, clearly making the point that our spirituality is not dependent on being religious!

Suggested words and themes include: joy, acceptance, love, power, forgiveness, surrender, communication, courage, peace, honesty, gratitude, hope. If we understand the challenge of spirituality as being the discovery of God in the world, meaningful relationships, the living of our lives, then we need to communicate a similar message in treatment. Some years ago, I rewrote Psalm 23 for patients in a treatment center. I also showed a prayer that I wrote for myself in recovery. Alongside the Lord's Prayer, let us encourage patients to write and create prayers and affirmations that are meaningful to them, using their own words and expressions to convey the God of their understanding, developing themes they consider important. Alongside gospel ballads, let us hear the popular songs of today's generation that express the spiritual themes of change, love, forgiveness, and acceptance. Let dance, music, art, poetry, literature, movies, and outside activities be used in presenting the concept of God. Only when we experience the challenge of life, life in its fullness, can the spiritual awakening be activated.

Spirituality in treatment concerns the healing of the whole body. The body, mind, and emotions all proclaim the God-given divinity of humankind; spirituality involves the whole person.

The tragedy in describing the human being as body, mind, and spirit is that it specifically separates the spirit (spirituality) from the activities that concern the body and mind. This has subconsciously predisposed people to think that spirituality involves prayer and meditation, but they tend not to connect spirituality with nutrition, sexuality, science, feelings, or jogging. This is tragic. Also, spirituality embraces the work of a medical doctor, nurse, physiotherapist, counselor, dietitian, cook, and visiting clergyperson who might conduct the spirituality lecture. Once this concept is understood in treatment and explained enthusiastically to patients, families, and employees, the miracle of recovery can comprehensively begin.

This diagram explains the concept:

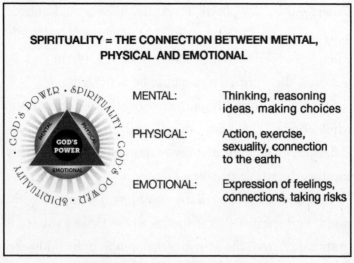

SPIRITUALITY = THE CONNECTION BETWEEN MENTAL, PHYSICAL AND EMOTIONAL

MENTAL: Thinking, reasoning ideas, making choices

PHYSICAL: Action, exercise, sexuality, connection to the earth

EMOTIONAL: Expression of feelings, connections, taking risks

SPIRITUALITY IS BEING FREE

The awareness of our dysfunctional behaviors creates the possibility for discovering our spiritual values. If we believe that in confronting what is unhealthy we are able to apprehend what needs to be done for recovery, developing the idea that in the acceptance of this disease are the seeds of wellness, then the miracle of treatment is realized. Spirituality is knowing that we have the power to change.

Spirituality is knowing that negatives can be turned into positives. I have provocatively suggested throughout this book that it is the acceptance and understanding of the disease that guides us into wellness; knowing what is wrong is the precondition for doing what is right. Spiritual power emerges in the admittance of our imperfections.

Let us put this idea to the test.

Disease Process

1. Unintelligible God
2. Denial
3. Dishonesty
4. Apathy/pessimism

5. Anger
6. Manipulation
7. Physical sickness
8. Isolation

9. Depression
10. Guilt/shame
11. Boredom
12. Fear

Spiritual Values

1. God as we understand God
2. Admittance/acceptance
3. Honesty
4. Energy/enthusiasm
5. Peace/serenity
6. Straightforwardness

7. Health
8. Involvement
9. Hope
10. Forgiveness/freedom
11. Joy in living
12. Self-confidence/esteem

I believe that the life of Jesus Christ and all the great religious and spiritual leaders revealed these spiritual values. When Jesus said, "I have come in order that you might have life—life in all its fullness" (John 10:10), Jesus was talking about realizing and expressing our "yes" to life. Treatment involves the development of these spiritual values that can be expressed in our recovering lives.

We have discovered the power to become positive and creative human beings.

In my book *Say Yes to Your Life: Daily Meditations for Recovery*, I describe the spiritual lifestyle in this way:

> Some things I seem to know intuitively: and I know that spirituality is involved in and affects everything. In a human being, it combines the physical, mental and emotional, but it also reaches beyond the human being and connects the peoples of the world. Spirituality is the force for good and wholeness in this universe.
>
> This is not just an opinion or thought. It is a feeling that runs so deep in my being that I know it must be true. When I read, hear music or see movies, this feeling is often evoked, and I know God is alive in this world and wanting it to be ONE.[12]

This is treatment.

Notes

1. Quoted in Leo Booth, *The Happy Heretic* (New York: Penguin Compas, 2002), 26.
2. Daniel Landinsky, *Love Poems from God* (New York: Penguin Books, 2002), 88.
3. Lore Cowan and Maurice Cowan, eds., *The Wit of the Jews* (London: Penguin Books, 1981), 47.
4. Margery Williams, *The Velveteen Rabbit* (New York: Avon Books, 1985), 12–13.
5. Jess Lair, *I Ain't Well, But I Sure Am Better* (New York: Doubleday, 1975), 91.
6. Alfred Alvarez, *The Shaping Spirit* (London: Chatto & Windus, 1957), 25.
7. Michael Howell and Peter Form, *The True History of the Elephant Man* (London: Penguin Books, 1980),189.
8. Ibid. 209.
9. Leo Booth, *Say Yes to Your Life* (Deerfield Beach: HCI, 2008), 197.
10. Alcoholics Anonymous, 4th ed. (New York: AA World Services, 2001).

About The Author

LEO BOOTH is a Unity Minister, a former Episcopal priest, and a recovering alcoholic. At the end of many years of heavy drinking, he was in a horrific car crash. That moment made him realize that life is too important to waste, so he checked himself into a treatment center.

Born in England, Leo came to the United States in 1981. Because of his personal experience with alcohol, he has dedicated his ministry toward recovery. His passion for helping other alcoholics and drug addicts inspired him to write *Say Yes to Life*, a daily meditation book that has sold more than 250,000 copies and has been republished as *Say Yes to Your Life*. His other titles include *The Angel and the Frog*, *The Wisdom of Letting Go*, *Say Yes to Your Spirit*, *Say Yes to Your Sexual Healing*, *Spirituality & Recovery*, and *The Happy Heretic*. He has appeared on national television shows including *Oprah* and *Good Morning America*. His spirituality articles appear in several recovery and health publications.

Leo continues counseling alcoholics and addicts in several treatment centers and presents spirituality seminars at conferences, mental health organizations, correctional facilities, and churches throughout the country. He is a certified addictions counselor and has written books on spirituality, compulsive behaviors, and sex addiction. To learn more visit www.fatherleo.com, or contact him at fatherleo@fatherleo.com. You can also read current insights and news events on Facebook: Reverend Leo Booth.